THE
FOREVER
MILLIONAIRE

DAVE SHEPHERD, CHFC, CFP®
DAVID W. SHEPHERD, JR., CFP®

THE
FOREVER
MILLIONAIRE

MAKING WISE CHOICES
———— WITH ————
YOUR WEALTH

Published by Advantage, Charleston, South Carolina.
Member of Advantage Media Group.

ADVANTAGE is a registered trademark, and the Advantage colophon is a trademark of Advantage Media Group, Inc.

Printed in the United States of America.

ISBN: 978-1-59932-753-2
LCCN: 2017931706

Cover design by Katie Biondo.

This publication is designed to provide accurate and authoritative information in regard to the subject matter covered. It is sold with the understanding that the publisher is not engaged in rendering legal, accounting, or other professional services. If legal advice or other expert assistance is required, the services of a competent professional person should be sought.

Advantage Media Group is proud to be a part of the Tree Neutral® program. Tree Neutral offsets the number of trees consumed in the production and printing of this book by taking proactive steps such as planting trees in direct proportion to the number of trees used to print books. To learn more about Tree Neutral, please visit **www.treeneutral.com.**

Advantage Media Group is a publisher of business, self-improvement, and professional development books. We help entrepreneurs, business leaders, and professionals share their Stories, Passion, and Knowledge to help others Learn & Grow. Do you have a manuscript or book idea that you would like us to consider for publishing? Please visit **advantagefamily.com** or call **1.866.775.1696.**

STOP!

Before you start reading this book, visit **theforevermillionaire.com**.

We've created the site specifically to help you put this book to work for you.

There you will find important tools and extra information that can help you start implementing the strategies outlined in this book, so it doesn't become a "someday" project.

Your finances deserve more than that. And most importantly, you and your loved ones deserve more too.

Go to **theforevermillionaire.com** NOW and let's get started! It's time to safeguard and grow your wealth—forever!

TABLE OF CONTENTS

THE BEST OF INTENTIONS

Can I trust you?

Are you going to screw me over like everybody else, or are you actually going to do something to help me?

A doctor told us that question is always on his mind when he's interviewing financial advisors. Do you have those same thoughts? Do you wonder how you can find someone to trust?

We have repeated those two questions in front of audiences in our workshops, and everybody nods and agrees.

"I just fired my advisor, and I'm looking for another one," a friend told us recently. "Now that I'm making more money, I want something more. All my advisor ever did was to have us fill out a standardized questionnaire and then put us into a standard portfolio that his firm offered."

Why do people feel like this? The first answer is because all too often it's true. There are many conflicts of interest, including behind-the-scenes payment schemes, incentive trips, and below-the-surface factors, that play into getting a poor result.

A number of people feel the problem is that their financial people are getting paid on commission. That's not the real problem. The real problem arises when the commission or fee is not transparent. It often is hidden and goes undiscussed, and as a result, you may not see its real effect on you.

You may have noticed that some voices on Wall Street and the financial industry suggest that there is never a bad time to invest. Why are they so bullish? Because their living depends on it. They want to sell the latest hot offering or promote the new merger and acquisition. They don't get paid because it does well or works out well—they get paid for selling it. And for that business to keep rolling, the markets have to be going up.

Another friend asked us recently about an advisor who "helps people grow their wealth." The advisor recommended that to grow the most wealth, she should pull her money out of her 401(k) and annually use the withdrawal to buy life insurance. Did we think that was a good idea? Besides the obvious tax issues, we told her it was not.

"Well, why would she recommend it?" our friend asked. We told her about commission differences between life insurance, annuities, and mutual funds. She asked why it mattered, since "you all get paid one way or another."

We made it plain to her: "A life insurance salesperson might get paid about $12,000 right now if you follow her advice. An annuity salesperson could get paid about $3,000. Your current mutual fund salesperson would get paid $1,500. Knowing that, do you see how salespeople have a financial incentive that affects what they recommend? When it isn't transparent how they are paid, it puts you in an awkward place."

Even if a salesperson claims to be unbiased and able to offer a range of products, you still do not know which of those might be offering the biggest commission or paying the most in fees, we explained. "That means that what is good for the salesperson might be worse for you." And she finally understood.

MY ADVISOR IS AWESOME!

We met recently with a woman who was raving about the quality of experienced advice that she and her husband had been getting. "My advisor is awesome. What makes you different?" she asked. We told her briefly about the "four seasons" of investing—a principle we believe in that most of our competition does not. You will learn much more about that in the pages ahead.

"Wow, my advisor doesn't do that," she said. "Basically what my advisor is doing is putting my money in the market, and the market is managing my money. You are actually talking about managing my money."

She told us that the advisor had also recommended that she and her husband, a developer, sell all their personal real estate holdings and put the money into real estate investment trusts (REITs) with the advisor. What did we think of that? We told her we believe the motive was simply to generate commissions. "That's what my husband said," she responded. No longer did their advisor seem so awesome to her.

From our experience many of today's big financial firms have a bottom-line culture. They sell proprietary products with special incentives, pushing to meet production quotas and corporate goals. They may be hyping a company's initial public offering, as they make a lot of money assisting with the stock sale, while their internal emails call it a less-than-stellar company. They were selling mortgage notes in 2005–2007 and touting their safety, while at the same time they were betting against them for their own accounts. Morningstar has reported that many money managers do not even invest in their own fund that they manage for you.[1] There can be many reasons they might not invest in their own fund, but would you feel better if they did? You can learn more about the industry's conflicts of interest in recent books including *Liar's Poker* and *The Big Short* by Michael Lewis. Or watch the movie version of *The Big Short*, recently an Oscar nominee for best picture.

Some of the industry, and the media that cover it, tell us simple "truths" that end up being only partial truths, which we will explore later in this book. For example, they tell us risk management (trying to protect against stock market losses when markets are declining) doesn't work but staying in the market all the time does—if you stay in the market and ride it out, you will average a certain return on investment. But the statistics show this: most investors spend about 60 percent of their time in the stock market trying to climb back to a previous high after a market decline—and that's assuming they don't sell out when the market is down.[2] Wouldn't it be better to know the whole truth and be able to prepare for it?

Markets and investing climates are unpredictable. If you really understood this one principle, you could take a different approach to managing risks. You could prepare for the unexpected and strive to do better when it happens. Some of the investments that "go bad" were ones where little was expected to go wrong. Sure, you can get any opinion you are looking for on the Internet or TV or from a salesperson. But in reality no one can predict the future.

---

1   Russel Kinnel, "Why You Should Invest with Managers Who Eat Their Own Cooking," Morningstar, March 31, 2015, http://www.morningstar.com/advisor/t/103820500/why-you-should-invest-with-managers-who-eat-their-own-cooking.htm.

2   standardsandpoors.com Sept. 2016

That unpredictable nature has much to do with why so many people distrust the industry and advisors. It also has the possibility of leading investors to make bad decisions. When they let their emotions get involved, they shoot themselves in the foot and hurt their own results. They chase investment gurus. When the market is being unpredictable, they look for who has been right or performed best lately. As a result, they often end up buying high and selling low—not the way to make money.

Studies have shown how such behavior dramatically affects results. When the market is peaking, more people are buying. When it is bottoming out, more people are selling. Look at what happened with housing in the 2000s. Very few people bought when prices were low. They started to buy only when they saw prices going up, and more people bought close to the top of the market. Then, when prices really fell, they stopped buying again.

It is a common pattern among investors; they chase returns and run from losses. The product providers and salespeople certainly understand the swing of emotions that leads people to buy high and sell low. You need to get off that roller coaster, which can lead you to do the wrong thing at the wrong time.

To keep emotions out of it and avoid bad decisions, some advisors suggest the strategy of buying and holding, despite the economic climate. In his recent book *Money*, Tony Robbins says he talked to his billionaire investor friends and that the sum of their wisdom for the average investor is to buy an "All-Weather Portfolio," and he gives his recommendations for it. We just wonder how many of those friends made their own money in such a portfolio. What if they didn't?

Why do billionaire investors invest one way and suggest the average person do it in a less sophisticated way? It's because some investors forget discipline when something goes wrong and let their emotions get involved and make decisions that may potentially hurt their returns, many times selling low and buying high. You don't have to do that to yourself after you learn a slightly different approach that we will outline for you here.

Our aim in this book is to give you the means to make wiser decisions. We will help you make the most of the time-tested and non-biased tools of financial planning and money management. We will help you rein in your own self-defeating emotions and avoid other people's self-serving advice that could lead you astray.

As an investor and consumer of financial services, you should remember three basics: (1) you need to know how to find someone you can trust who will be more like a partner than a salesperson, (2) you need transparency about what motivates the advisor and how he or she is paid, and (3) you need to overcome half-truths and use strategies that can help you stay off that scary emotional roller coaster as markets rise and fall.

Throughout the book, we will give you information, ideas, and fresh thinking on how you can interact with your current advisor, look for a new advisor, or potentially do things better yourself. You will find helpful ideas here whether you are building toward an eventual retirement or have already crossed that threshold. In this book we may use *retirement, financial stability,* and *financial freedom* as interchangeable terms. Some people have jobs they want to retire from and never work again. Others are currently looking for financial stability and the freedom to do what they want, when they want. Regardless of how you look at it, we are striving to enhance your freedom to achieve what is important to you.

It's not our purpose here to write a complete guide examining every angle of financial planning. You will find many such financial books on a wide variety of topics at your bookstore and online, and they adequately address the fundamentals—or you can search for information on the Internet, to the extent that you can trust the sources. Rather, we want to emphasize the essential nature of comprehensive planning and how all those topics must interrelate if you are to pursue success.

This is the thread that you will find interwoven in these chapters: the need to create order out of what so easily can turn to chaos. A clear and intentional plan that guides your decisions will bring you confidence as you do better in your financial life.

It is time to know more, be wiser, and do better.

WE BELIEVE . . .

1. That everyone needs a "trusted advisor" who is not seen as a salesperson. Our clients should be educated in an unbiased way so that, with trust and mutual understanding, we can work better together as we strive to achieve better results.

2. That a financial planning process should be the basis for all decisions. Having a process that can be reviewed and updated (a living plan) should shape future decisions. No "drive-by" advice.

3. That we should have a process for making sure all details are checked and kept up to date so a client's financial life is always in order.

4. That we should have a process for anticipating and proactively meeting all the needs and potential needs of our clients.

5. That one of our most important roles is being a constant source of support, up to date and familiar

with all details, so that we can be there for our clients—especially a surviving spouse. We want to have the full faith and trust of that spouse so we can carry on the plans and strategies we have laid out.

6.   That it is crucial to be in a position to offer unbiased advice, no corporate pressure or sales quotas, and an open system for finding appropriate products and strategies for each client. We want to facilitate whatever solution is necessary and appropriate for each circumstance.

7.   In diversification of investment strategies, because every strategy will have a time of underperformance.

8.   That risk and opportunity change over time and that preserving portfolios from loss is just as important as participating in a market advance. We know that markets and the future are unpredictable and that we must constantly be diligent by paying attention, learning, and improving.

9.   That the most important discipline of investing is in picking a strategy and sticking with it. Jumping from underperforming to "what is doing better" in many cases helps us to sell low and buy high, hurting long-term performance.

10.   That to the extent we are able to help make investing a more comfortable, less emotional experience, the entire plan will be easier to stick with, potentially leading to better results.

CHAPTER 1

IT STARTS WITH TRUST

A friend who educates and trains financial advisors related a story he'd heard from a business owner seated next to him on a flight about his experience in trying to find a financial advisor.

This business owner was fairly prosperous, with about half of his net worth in a small, upscale resort chain and the other half in normal liquid investments such as stocks, bonds, and certificates of deposit. He realized that you need expert help with your important business dealings, tax management, and family security issues. He was looking for a competent and trustworthy advisor to simplify life in today's complex financial world.

Three friends had each given him a referral, and he interviewed the potential candidates. All three left him feeling disappointed. They offered the same sort of advice, and it all seemed to be just about the money. Frankly, it didn't seem as if they cared much about him. They didn't take the time to ask about his unique situation, how and why he wanted what he wanted. In the end, they each proposed almost the same generic investment asset allocation program, which they assured him was the perfect pie chart of an optimum portfolio. Nonetheless, it just didn't seem tailored to meet his wishes or needs.

Each of the three advisors suggested that he sell all his real estate holdings that he'd spent half a lifetime accumulating and that he transfer the money into real estate investment trusts with the advisor. It seemed that this "advice" was not necessarily what would be best for him but rather what would be best for the advisor's wallet.

That is the general experience that so many new clients have described when they come to us. Some of the financial industry is built around ensuring that *it* makes money, not that *you* make money. Salespeople will suggest something that at best is simply suitable for you and then will try to convince you that you need it.

If that investor had been our client, he would have found our approach to be quite different. We would have first precisely identified the outcomes he wanted for his family, reviewing all the relevant information. We would have examined whether what he already owned was working well—after all, privately owned real estate can be a great asset if you are comfortable with managing it. We would have determined just where he wanted help and then suggested options that might fill those gaps, weighing all the trade-offs. And we would have established a checklist and review process to keep it all clear.

That is the kind of experience that builds trust. The job of a good advisor is to help clients strive toward their goals. They need someone who is firmly on their side. That is the only basis for a relationship that will last.

"Do as I Say, Not as I Do"

A couple who recently came to see us had lost a lot of money in oil and gas pipeline investments that they had been told were relatively safe. After the investments declined 25 percent, the couple went to their advisor. He suggested that they just hang on and that the investments would rebound. They did not. They lost more money.

They called the advisor again, worried about how much the investment had declined. It had fallen 50 percent in value from the point when they had purchased it. "You definitely want to ride this out!" the advisor told the couple. "At these prices, hey, *even I* am interested in buying some of that!"

Consider that a glimpse into the kind of thinking that is common on Wall Street. Wall Street has a long history of coming up with products and a reasonable-sounding story/sales pitch for them. Once, nursing home bonds were the rage and considered a sure thing—after all, people were getting older, weren't they? Many of those investments went broke, returning nothing or much less than expected. In the 1980s, we had limited partnerships and tax shelters, oil and gas partnerships, real estate partnerships, life insurance cash value schemes, and junk bonds. Let's not forget Michael Milken. And in the late 1990s, we saw Wall Street firms pumping Internet stocks to the public at the same time that the brokers themselves were calling them dogs and losers in their emails. We soon learned why, as the market crashed and many of those stocks became worthless.

Salespeople do not always do what they recommend, It's an attitude of "do as I say, not as I do"—and that's hardly the way to build trust.

DRIVE-BY ADVICE

—Dave

For a number of years I have employed the term "drive-by advice" when referring to the less-than-genuine recommendations that characterize so much of the financial industry. Let me explain how I coined that phrase—and as you will see, it started out rather literally.

Several years ago, I had my heart set on buying a boat. It was a beauty, a twenty-six-foot Cobalt ski boat, and I had been transferring money into my checking account so that I could get a certified check for the boat dealer.

One day as I was at the drive-through window making my last deposit before the purchase, the teller had a question for me: "Would you like to come in and talk to one of our associates? I see that you have built up a considerable amount in your checking account, and we probably could suggest a better way to put that money to use…"

"No thanks, I am just parking the money here because I am going to buy a boat," I told her.

Four years later, my wife and I decided to sell the boat, because by that time we had small grandchildren who weren't going to be swimming anytime soon, much less waterskiing—and the allure of going to the lake was not as strong if our grandkids wouldn't be there. We figured we would sell this boat and get another when they got older.

After selling the boat, we had a sizable check to temporarily deposit. This time, it was my wife who approached the drive-through teller, who dutifully handled the transaction—and then added: "With that much money in your checking account, you really ought to see one of our associates…"

That teller was just doing her job, of course, but there's an important lesson there: when people see that you have investable cash, they often are quick to offer you some kind of drive-by advice. By that I mean they dispense advice on the fly, without finding out much about you, your needs, or your goals. They see an opportunity to make money by using your money, and for the most part that is simply the way the industry operates. I am sure that if my wife or I had gone through those bank doors to talk to that associate, he or she would not have wanted to do the work of a comprehensive overall financial picture, nor would he or she have taken the time to build a holistic, comprehensive plan for us based on our situation and aspirations.

All too often, consumers are ready to jump at such drive-by advice. Perhaps a couple find themselves with $500,000 saved up, or it comes to them as a windfall—and what should they do with it? Often they look for a short-term solution, and when someone at the bank says, "Hey, step into the back office," it sounds like a good idea. Or an insurance agent offers them other ideas on how the money could be used. Or they get a flyer in the mail inviting them to a seminar on annuities.

It's all so tempting. They want to solve that "problem" of what to do with the money, and they will find no shortage of opinions as to where it should go. They need to talk with someone who will look at their entire situation and make sure that whatever they do with the money fits in appropriately with their long-term goals. A drive-by won't do.

Distortions of the Truth

Think about how much more efficiently you shop for groceries if you have a recipe in mind. When you focus on that nourishing meal you intend to make and what must go into it, you are less likely to reach for things you do not particularly need and that would not be good for you.

We also suggest that you make your financial decisions with a "recipe" in mind, knowing exactly what you will need and where it will fit in your plan. Begin with the end in mind, clearly identifying what you want the outcome to be, and then add what it will take to get you to that goal.

You should be working with an advisor who takes the time to understand you and your needs and goals and doesn't simply give a sales pitch with an easy, off-the-shelf solution. We see it like this: people have legitimate worries and desires about their future and how the markets might affect it. To reduce those worries requires thoughtful planning, looking at all available alternatives and monitoring continually. For good results, you need much more than the Band-Aid of a quick, commissioned product sale.

Unfortunately, many people are eager to hear a good story and are not really looking for comprehensive advice. It is human nature to want an easy fix, and those talking heads on television and the commentators in the financial media have plenty to say about what investors should or should not be buying or selling or doing. The media people want to capture an audience, and they know that appealing to emotions is a good way to get attention. Meanwhile, the salespeople know that appealing to emotions is a good way to get the commission.

There are many stories like these in circulation. They are myths or half-truths. For example, one of the pieces of "wisdom" promoted by media and money management firms goes like this: *You need to stay invested no matter what. Market timing doesn't work, and if you missed the ten best days of market returns over the last ten years, you give up half your return. Never get out!*

But as Russell Investments pointed out in a recent blog post (July 19, 2016, on blog.helpingadvisors.com), it is also true that if you missed the ten worst days of the last ten years, you doubled your return. We are not arguing for market timing by any means. But if you hear only one side of a "fact," you could be at risk of changing your behavior and failing to do risk management.

And here is the problem. We mentioned earlier that since 1929, through all the ups and downs of the markets, about 60 percent (data in chapter 5) of the time if you stay invested during a downturn you are just working to recoup your losses. If that stat holds true, then 60 percent of the time you want to be retired or financially free, your investments could be working just to get back to a previous market high. Does that make sense to you? Will playing catch-up most of the time make you feel secure or financially free?

The media are quick to report such sound bites from the experts, thereby promoting the myths to the point where they become common knowledge. Prevailing beliefs, however, are not tantamount to wisdom. Most people perceive that the media dispense advice for the masses. In reality, the media will do whatever is necessary to keep your attention so they can sell advertising, and their stories may be favorable to their biggest advertisers. (Or are we just being cynical?) They do not know you as an individual and therefore can only provide generic information that, by its nature, may not serve you well.

We made regular appearances on CNBC for a while but became frustrated when it became apparent that the network was not a forum where we could provide meaningful advice. Our first appearance, back in 2009, happened to be on the day the Dow finally crossed 10,000 again on its way back up. It was a party atmosphere. We suggested caution, pointing out how many times the Dow had already crossed that point—and, just like that, we were off the air and they had gone on to something else. It seems what we had to say was counter to the point they were trying to make that particular day.

The point is that the stories that people so readily believe are powerful because they are emotive, and your money decisions should not be based on emotion unless you are making a charitable donation from the heart. Financial decisions need to be rational, impartial, and based on the facts as they pertain to your personal situation.

SALES TACTICS

In his classic book *Influence: The Psychology of Persuasion*, Robert Cialdini describes compliance (or persuasion) tactics by which companies—and that includes those in the finance industry—get consumers to make decisions about parting with their money. Here are some of those tactics, which you might well recognize since they are the substance of sales pitches everywhere:

Consistency: If you commit to something on a small level, you are more likely to remain committed to it in a later decision at a larger level.

Reciprocity: If somebody has offered you something, you tend to get a feeling of obligation and in some way want to return the favor.

Social proof: You tend to be influenced by what people similar to you are doing. That is why commercials portray people in the demographic that they are targeting.

Peer following: You tend to follow the crowd, which is a human tendency that advertisers and finance companies use to full advantage.

Authority: You feel a sense of obligation and duty to people who are recognized or perceived as authoritative in their positions. That is why "doctors recommend" has long been a common phrase in pharmaceutical advertisements, for example. One pharmaceutical ad used an actor who played a physician on a television show—he wasn't even a doctor in real life—and he generated so much authority it was one of the best pharmaceutical ads of all time.

Likability: You are more likely to be influenced by people you like.

Scarcity: If you think you are going to miss out on an opportunity, you are more likely to go after it. When you perceive that something of value will become hard to get, you feel all the more motivated to pursue it.

Exclusivity: This is similar to scarcity in that you want to feel as if you are getting an opportunity that is not offered to others. You are getting a special deal by virtue of someone you know, something you have done, or something you have joined.

It is virtually a certainty that at some point you have been the target of a pitch that used one or probably more of these tactics to persuade you to take action. Perhaps you have been invited to one of those "free dinner" seminars at a nice restaurant in which the only topic of conversation is annuities or other high commission products. Think about the compliance tactics involved. The host represents himself or herself as an authority. The free meal tends to make you feel obligated to do something in return, whether you reciprocate by purchasing the product or by at least setting up an appointment. The presentation probably uses the tactic of social proof, with a video or slideshow of enthusiastic and engaged people looking much like you and those around you.

Many such events have come from the quota-driven Wall Street sales culture. Typically, salespeople offer their company's products that could generate a higher commission for the companies and themselves. Those products might be suitable for some of those attending, but they are not necessarily in their best interests. Salespeople have long been trained to find a prospect's pain points and emphasize that pain to persuade him or her to buy something perceived as a means to relieve it.

Finding Unbiased Advice

Many in the industry would heartily agree that you need to find unbiased advice, but it's not as simple as that. There is really no escaping bias. Certainly you want to avoid the kind of bias that seeks to blind you to the options that are available to you, but an advisor's "bias" can simply be the reflection of what he or she truly believes. You deserve clear and impartial advice, but finding it is easier said than done. You'll want to avoid self-serving bias, of course, but also make sure an advisor's belief matches up with yours.

An important consideration is whether you are dealing with someone who holds to a fiduciary standard, which requires advisors to always act in the best interests of their clients. They must put the client's well-being ahead of their own. For example, fiduciary advisors cannot buy securities for their personal accounts before purchasing those same securities on behalf of their clients, and they cannot make trades for the sake of bringing in higher commissions for themselves or the investment firm. They must disclose any potential conflict of interest and do their best to offer advice based on accurate and complete information. This is what Department of Labor (DOL) rules are aimed at doing for consumers with retirement accounts.

We believe fiduciary advisors, in other words, are held to a standard of loyalty and care similar to that which a doctor or a lawyer or accountant is expected to provide to clients. Broker-dealers, historically, have only been required to fulfill a suitability obligation—they only had to reasonably believe that their suggestions and products would be suitable for the client, even if they were not necessarily in the client's best interests (the fiduciary standard). Their loyalty, however, was not foremost to the client. Their first duty was to the financial house that employed them, and therefore their interests were not necessarily aligned with the client's. The DOL rules aim to level the playing field and make them accountable to the fiduciary standard.

Fiduciary vs. Suitability Standard

	FIDUCIARY	SUITABILITY
DUTY OF LOYALTY	To client	To firm and client
CONFLICTS OF INTEREST	Avoid and disclose	Not as strict as fiduciary standard
PRIMARY CONCERN	Best solution	Suitable solution
COSTS	Transparent	Opaque
USE OF HIGHER COMPENSATION ALTERNATIVE	Prohibited	Allowed

The fiduciary standard is one difference between a salesperson and an advisor. A second difference is the belief in comprehensive advice instead of drive-by advice. A new client recently told us he would soon have an additional $100,000 to invest as we were working on his plan. We told him, "Let's finish up what we are working on and that will tell us where that money should go in your plan."

"Now I get it!" he responded. "If I had told my old broker that, I wouldn't have been able to write the check fast enough for him. He always had something to sell me but never wanted to do any real planning."

Often at a seminar or workshop, you will find salespeople ready to pitch you on a product that will pay them handsomely if they can get you to buy it. We, too, can advise you on annuities and life insurance when those make sense for you, but our approach is different. We help you shop for an appropriate solution, and for us it's not about generating commissions. It's about how the solution fits in with your overall best interests. We take a global view of your financial situation, brainstorming and considering the potential outcomes of various scenarios and solutions in the marketplace, and then we continue the relationship over the years. If your situation changes, we help you adjust or start anew.

When we act as fiduciaries, we don't make our money up front in a transaction. You pay us a clearly defined fee for the experience, knowledge, and advice that we provide you long term. Our compensation is not hidden within some product. A commission-based salesperson might make $40,000 to $120,000, depending on the product, on every million dollars you invest. Because you don't see it you don't know what incentive or bias may have been a part of why it was recommended. Our incentive is to understand your needs and then grow and protect your assets. We want to transform the way people do business.

A HEART FOR PEOPLE

—Dave

For three weeks when I was a young man, I sold cars at a small dealership in Tucson. I learned a lot in that short time. In fact, I found a piece to my puzzle that launched a successful career.

The reason my stint as a car salesman was so short was that I found that the sales managers did not treat either the customers or the sales staff honorably. They insisted that we "bump" the customer at least three times—by persuading them that they had to pay more, or selling them something additional, such as a warranty. It felt adversarial, as if I wasn't helping someone but rather competing with them over their money.

By the end of those three weeks, customers were already returning and asking for me by name. One older man waited two hours for me, refusing to talk to any of the other salespeople who were eager to deliver their pitch. The managers had trained us to get potential buyers in a room and hammer at them and not let them get away, but I had not taken that approach with that particular gentleman. Instead, I'd told him, "Well, give it some thought, and if you would like to come back and talk, anytime." He told me he liked me because I wasn't pushy and because I was trying to help him instead of compelling him to buy a car. And so he bought a car.

Later I went to work for an insurance agency, focusing on clients who were sixty-five or older. At the time, I was just starting a family: We had a six-month-old boy, David. We were living with my mother-in-law and trying to make ends meet. Within a year, I became a top selling agent for that company nationwide—but I soon found that I was seeing little of my family. I was heading out to work before our baby woke up and getting home long past his bedtime. I started to think about what mattered most to me. What was the real meaning of success?

I know now that my early success there was because I was in a role that suited me well. I was able to be the trusted advisor, and my job was not to sell so much as it was to tell. My aim was to educate people so they could make the best decisions for themselves. I explained to older people their options and what was available to them. And I found, at age twenty-four, that they wanted to help me as well. It's as if they viewed me as a grandson. I would proudly show them pictures of David at six months, and the conversation would range over topics far beyond insurance. And when we did return to talking about the matter at hand, they found it easy to trust me.

As salespeople though, we were trained to make pitches that I did not feel were in the clients' best interests. Once, a manager helped me sell a policy that would have earned me a $5,000 commission—but my client was uncomfortable and changed her mind. I had to fight with the hierarchy to get her money back. As a young family we could have used that $5,000, and it hurt to give it back—but it was the right thing to do. Thirty-three years later, she is ninety years old and remains a loyal client and friend. Doing the right thing has always paid off for us.

Three years later, though, I faced a disappointment. The first long-term care policies were coming out then, and I was asked to offer one that I considered to be inferior. I wanted to offer clients what I knew was far better coverage from another company, but I felt pressured to sell the favored policy—or else. I left to start my own company where I would be able to access the best products for those who placed their trust in me.

Later, as an investment advisor, I had a choice with which financial firm I wanted my clients' accounts to be held at. I found myself in another situation where I had to switch financial firms when a larger company bought out the firm I had client accounts at and began heavily promoting its own products. If a salesperson did not sell the proprietary products, he or she would not get the best pay, or the best office, or the best benefits.

In the end, what I learned from both my abbreviated career as a car salesman and my years working in someone else's agency was that I couldn't offer second best like other sales-people. What I cherished was being a trusted advisor. And I learned something else: I really had a knack for working with older people. Over the years, they have grown weary of games. They want assistance, but they don't like to be sold. And as a man who likes to assist but doesn't like to sell, I decided that the time had come to strike out on my own.

A third difference between a salesperson and an advisor is that an advisor has access to a broad range of solutions and can use outside experts if needed without any corporate pressure, incentives, or quotas.

In our experience, an independent business owner who works directly with clients inhabits a far different environment than the advisor who is an employee of a large firm. Large companies are run top-down. The pay, bonuses, and incentives are designed to meet corporate goals and production quotas. In our firm, we have no such corporate agenda, bottom line, or product and strategy preferences.

We are investment advisor representatives (IARs) with an independent registered investment advisor RIA.

The structure of our firm is what is known in the industry as a hybrid: most of our business is fee-based, although we still have an affiliation with a broker-dealer firm for commissioned transactions involving more traditional types of products. That flexibility helps us to service our legacy clients and offer a broad range of appropriate strategies—and sometimes it can actually be less expensive to pay a commission. For example, if you are buying municipal bonds to hold for ten or fifteen years, you probably would rather pay a one-time commission than pay a continuing advisory fee. Also, some products are only available on a commission basis—long-term care insurance, for example. We don't want to send a client out into the marketplace to shop when we can use a shopping service, narrow down the best available choices, and review them with the client and take care of everything including being an advocate if the client has a claim.

Almost always, except for age and risk level differences, what we recommend to clients is what we own ourselves. Under the fiduciary standard, when we make any buy or sell or similar change, everybody is traded at the same time and gets the same price, including ourselves.

To get truly comprehensive advice, we and our clients frequently need to consult with other professionals, whom we can bring into the conversation whenever appropriate. Those subject matter experts need to collaborate not only with us but also with the client. We have often accompanied clients when they meet with an attorney, and many times we have been able to help them more fully understand the significance and implications of what we are doing. Lawyers and other experts sometimes talk in legalese, and we can help to interpret so that our clients maintain a perspective on their overall financial picture.

Are You a DIYer?

Some people believe they can handle their investments and financial planning on their own, and they feel empowered by all the free advice that swirls around us in this Internet age. It has become easier and easier, for example, to pick out a mutual fund. Like other media, however, the Internet does not offer advice that is tailored for the individual, and it is difficult to avoid getting buried by such an avalanche of information and opinions. We'll show later how the most popular beliefs are not even the best performing.

Many people don't want to personally coordinate all their complex financial affairs. They need to balance all the legal and tax and investment considerations into a cohesive whole. There are so many decisions to be made, one after another: Which pension option is best? What is the best age to begin receiving a Social Security benefit? Which investments are best for a particular situation, and how should they be handled from a tax perspective? How can estate matters be handled in fairness to all the children in a blended family?

And what is the best way to design the financial plan to anticipate the inevitability of declining health? If the spouse who handles all the financial affairs becomes physically or mentally unable to do so, a couple's financial plan can fall apart because the coordinator can no longer keep it together. What happens in that case to the do-it-yourself plan? The spouse who has paid little attention to financial issues is forced to go it alone, and someone could easily take advantage of that situation.

That is why a trusted financial advisor is so crucial in developing strategies that will endure for decades to come. This is not a matter of picking out a mutual fund or signing some document. Those are important matters, but isolated actions do not add up to success. All the elements of a financial plan must work well together and make sense comprehensively.

Decisions, Decisions

You need to be aware of the cognitive fallacies that can distort how you look at things. Nobel laureate Daniel Kahneman, author of *Thinking, Fast and Slow*, details such concepts as anchoring, availability bias, substitution, optimism, loss aversion, framing, and sunk costs.

Here's why you should care: those common distortions of reasoning could have a massive impact on your financial success and investment results over time.

Financial decision making is incredibly complex, involving forks in the road and trade-offs that compound one another. The brain is complex as well, but it can play tricks. When you are aware of those tricks, you can make better financial decisions. Here's a brief look at the fallacies that Kahneman describes:

- *Anchoring* is the tendency to make questionable assessments based on what has been experienced recently. An investment example would be: "I bought this for $70 a share. It's fallen to $60 a share. I am not selling it until it gets back to $70."

- *Availability bias* describes the inclination to base decisions on what is in front of you at the moment. There's a saying that goes "What you see is all there is." You tend to evaluate other options less well when you aren't looking at them or don't know they exist.

- *Substitution* is the tendency to substitute and answer a simpler question when a more complex one is presented. In doing so, you jump to conclusions and are likely to arrive at the wrong answer.

- *Optimism,* in the sense of a cognitive fallacy, is the tendency to be overly assured of our own ability to influence outcomes.

Unwarranted optimism can lead to taking big risks without accurately calculating the odds of success.

- *Loss aversion* describes the inclination to fear loss more than to desire gain. This leads to passing over good opportunities where the odds of winning are highly favorable.

- *Framing* is the tendency to make decisions based on how the situation is presented. Surgery with a 90 percent survival rate seems safer than surgery with a 10 percent mortality rate. Describing food as 95 percent fat-free makes it sound more healthful than saying it contains 5 percent fat.

- *Sunk costs* are the result of throwing good money after bad or staying in a bad situation such as an unfulfilling career or abusive relationship. Some tend to worry that they will be perceived as failures if they admit a mistake and cut their losses.

Now let's think about those concepts when it comes to your money. Have you ever had a losing investment but couldn't bring yourself to sell it because it was worth so much more when you bought it not that long ago? That's anchoring and sunk costs at work. What if someone were to tell you that a particular investment paid 8 percent in income? Sound good? That's framing.

An example of substitution could be considering the question of "Do I want the one that pays 5 percent or the one that pays 6 percent?" without considering the larger questions, which are "What are the chances for getting my principle back, how long will it take, and does that fit in with my financial plan and needs?" Consider what you are not being told, such as that the underlying securities are extremely risky and could decimate your principal.

Your underlying personality also could have much to do with how you make decisions. In her book *Quiet: The Power of Introverts in a World That Can't Stop Talking*, Susan Cain examines some of those differences. Extroverts tend to communicate quickly and effectively as they focus on the relationship aspects. They also tend to feel a rush from taking risks. In their decisions, they do not easily separate themselves from their emotions. Introverts can do so more readily, using reason and slowing down to take corrective action.

The logical conclusion seems to be that you would be more likely to trust an introvert to manage your money. The extroverts would not necessarily be the best for that job, although they are the ones who tend to get the attention because they are better at relating. Those are broad generalities but something to consider.

The bottom line is this: Not all our brains are wired the same, and that's a good thing—but you must be aware of it. It's often said that you can trust no one better than yourself, but standing alone you are more susceptible to your inherent weaknesses. We each must examine our motivations and consult with others who might offer perspectives that we haven't considered.

Every individual will have a different approach to his or her financial life. That is why it is so important to understand the under-pinnings of decision making and the psychology of investment and the many other aspects of comprehensive financial planning. You need to be working with someone in a long-term relationship who understands you and your family and the goals that you have dreamed about for so long. It starts with trust, and it builds from there, through good times and bad, as the bulls and the bears come and go. Both client and advisor have a responsibility for maintaining a committed relationship that will endure for decades.

——————— T H I N K I N G   P O I N T S ———————

1. Is your advisor a fiduciary?

2. Does your advisor believe in comprehensive planning? Do you?

3. Does your advisor have expertise and access to a broad range of solutions? What are they?

4. Does your advisor work for you or for their employer?

CHAPTER 2

BUILDING YOUR PLAN

If you have ever felt you were going in circles trying to deal with all of life's challenges and priorities, you are not alone. Most of us worry that we will miss something minor along the way that could make a big difference. You need a clear destination and guideposts to get there.

Without those references, in fact, people literally do walk in circles, scientists have discovered. Scientists led by Jan Souman at the Max Planck Institute for Biological Cybernetics in Germany conducted experiments in which they put people in unfamiliar forests and deserts and tracked them by GPS. The expectation was that the subjects would walk in random directions, but what they discovered was that the subjects indeed often walked in circles. Only if the sun, moon, or other reference point was visible could they walk in a straight line; if it was cloudy, they often resorted to circles, suggesting consistent errors rather than random ones.[3]

The same can happen with you and your hard-earned money. Just as sailors need a lighthouse, you need a clear frame of reference to guide you through the haze. Otherwise you could make the same mistakes over and over again. Investors tend to sell low and buy high, for example, and without good guidance they may follow that pattern

---

3   J.L. Souman, I. Frissen, M.N. Sreenivasa, and M.O. Ernst, "Walking straight into circles," *Current Biology* 19, no. 18 (2009): 1538-42.

repeatedly. Disappointed when an investment isn't working out, they sell it at a loss and then look for whatever is hot at the moment to replace it. They wander in the woods, slog through swamps, and end up back where they started and certainly far from where they wanted to go.

Direction and Destination

The lesson is this: You need a plan that is clear and intentional so that you can learn from your mistakes and find your way back to solid ground. You need a reference point in the distance that will help guide your decisions and actions for a more direct path to your goals. You need clear guidelines to stay focused on the outcomes most important to you.

Here are four planning considerations that will help your understanding:

1. Planning is not just about figuring out how to save a million dollars. It is about checking and double checking how all the complex elements of your financial life interrelate. Like magnets, those elements can either attract or repel depending on how they are positioned.

2. It is also about periodically reviewing and adjusting to changes in your life, as well as in the markets, tax structure, and regulations.

3. The process of planning helps your advisor understand you better—and helps you understand yourself—so that together you can take specific actions to get to specific goals.

4. You and your advisor need to be committed to the time and effort required. If either of you fails to grasp that, the planning will fail.

When people first come to us, they often have decided they want a laser focus on their most important goals. They may be getting closer to the point of retirement, desiring financial stability and freedom and wondering whether they have accomplished enough. They may lack clarity.

Most of them have saved well and at least have a great start toward their financial independence. In fact, they generally are financially sophisticated but are looking to delegate the day-to-day tasks to someone else. We help them clarify how much work remains to be done. We make sure that they are fully aware of any deeper issues that lie beneath the surface.

Once they gain clarity about their destination, they are able to map out the way to get there. With a clear goal in mind, they can take all the appropriate steps. In the words of entrepreneur and author Jim Rohn: "If you don't design your own life plan, chances are you'll fall into someone else's plan. And guess what they have planned for you? Not much."

The Steps of a True Plan

Years ago, professional financial planning was a rarity in the industry. Basically, salespeople for the major financial institutions sold their company's products to their clients and did the minimum amount of planning necessary to get commissions.

With the rise in popularity of the Certified Financial Planner™ (CFP®) designation, however, some of those big firms began to see planning as a revenue source. They actually had quotas for their advisors to do plans. Each representative would have to do so many a month, and the company charged for that service. The companies wanted to follow the trend, but eventually the financial planning fell by the wayside as they recognized that the real money was in managing a lot of money or selling their various products.

Financial planning has gone through waves of popularity—sometimes offered for free, sometimes for a fee. Today, the major firms will conduct financial planning, but it is the minimum needed to get assets under management—which is where they make their money. They are not primarily in the business of providing comprehensive advice.

The CFP® guidelines list six steps in seeking financial advice: (1) establish a relationship with a CFP® professional, (2) gather your data and develop your financial goals, (3) analyze and evaluate your financial status, (4) review the CFP® professional's recommendations, (5) set the course, and (6) benchmark your progress against the financial goals you established.

Here, in three steps, is a simpler way to look at it: (1) examine your current situation, (2) set your financial goals, and (3) measure your progress. Those other six steps certainly are important guidelines, but these three distill them to the essentials. They amount to the framework for putting a plan together and executing it effectively.

Getting to the Why

Along with those steps, your advisor needs to uncover your "why" to help you get where you want to go. The "what" is your destination—your desired goals and outcome. Your planning strategies are your "how." But the "why" is the fuel that will get you there.

We cannot emphasize enough how essential it is to begin with the end in mind. In fact, that is your single most important stake in the ground, and we spend time with our clients helping them to focus on life priorities before we get to the nuts and bolts of finances and investments.

In his book *First Things First*, Stephen R. Covey tells a story about dealing with priorities that goes something like this: An old professor is lecturing on efficient time management. On the table in front of him is a large glass jar. Next to it are about a dozen fist-size rocks, which he places, one by one, into the jar until no more will fit.

"Is the jar full?" he asks the class, and the students tell him it most certainly is full. The professor then pulls a bucket of gravel from under the table and pours some of it into the jar, shaking it so that the gravel works its way among the rocks.

Again he asks: "Is the jar full?" The class hesitates. "Probably not," a student offers, and the professor nods as he pulls out a bucket of sand, pouring some of it into the jar, as well. The sand settles into much of the remaining space.

"How about now—is it full?" the old professor asks, and as the class shouts "*No!*" he lifts a pitcher and fills the jar to the brim with water. He asks the students what they have learned from this demonstration. "Does it mean you can always cram one more thing into your day?" one student asks.

"No," the professor said. "It means that if you don't get the big rocks into place first, you'll never be able to make them fit."

Everyone has their own big rocks that they should be striving to get into place first. Perhaps the rocks represent family, or health, or fighting for a cause, or reaching for personal goals—the list differs for everyone, but whatever they are, you must not let the smaller things, the ones that tend to preoccupy us, get in the way of those priorities. Unless you plan out your life, the gravel and the sand will certainly fill up your jar until there is no room for the rocks anymore. You should attend first to the fundamentals and then let the details fall into place.

Many people have not paused long enough to identify what those big rocks in their lives might be. When we talk to couples about their dreams, it sometimes seems as if they have not thought about them for years. Life gets in the way. It's easy to say, "You need to set goals, and begin with the end in mind." But how, in practice, do you determine what matters most to you when it seems that so many things are of such pressing concern?

One way is the concept of "bubble sorting," as described by Keith Ellis in his book *The Magic Lamp: Goal Setting for People Who Hate Setting Goals.* First, jot down a wish list of things that you would like to accomplish in life or that you would like to get from life. Your list will be in no particular order of priority. When you are done, number them in the order that you wrote them. Then look at numbers one and two and decide which is more important to you, labeling that one as "current choice." Compare that to number three, deciding which of those two should become your current choice. Then move on to number four, again choosing which is most important to you.

1. _____

2. _____

3. _____

4. _____

5. _____

6. _____

7. _____

8. _____

9. _____

10. _____

As you work your way down the list, you will be constantly reevaluating your current choice. By the time you are done, your most important goal will, in effect, have bubbled up to the top. You have compared everything on the list, and you have identified your number-one priority. Next, consider the remaining items, going through the same process: Compare the item that is now second on your list against the next and choose a preference, then compare it with the next item on the list, and so on. Soon your number-two goal will have bubbled up, and you can start again with the remaining items. Eventually you will have prioritized your entire list.

1. _____

2. _____

3. _____

4. _____

5. _____

6. _____

7. _____

8. _____

9. _____

10. _____

A STRATEGY FOR SUCCESS

—David

I've been involved in a program called Strategic Coach, founded by Dan Sullivan and Babs Smith, designed to help us identify our most important goals and forge and execute a path to a bigger future. Every quarter, we set and review goals and track our progress.

As part of the program, I have a coach who has worked with me to set six categories of values and goals within each of those categories. The ones that I have identified are: God, spouse, kids, health, relationships, and "unique ability"—that is, what each of us was uniquely put here to do.

Such goal setting is of great value when life gets busy. We all get to the point where we have to decide among competing activities and endeavors. When we have identified our life priorities in advance, we are in a much better position to choose. Each of the results that I am trying to accomplish in each of those six areas is very important to me, but in the course of a day or a week they sometimes can conflict with one another. Since the priorities have been intentionally set in advance, the one with the higher priority wins out.

It's an exercise that anyone would be wise to try. By having a clear grasp of your values, and sorting them out by priority, you will spend less time wondering what you should do. You will be able to proceed with confidence, knowing that you have seen the big picture.

It's not enough simply to identify your end goals. You need to understand in your heart why those goals are so important to you. Sometimes people believe that they must accomplish something, but when they examine the "why" of the matter, they come to see that perhaps some things really are not worth focusing on or perhaps they are pursuing them for the wrong reasons. Sometimes people end up living the life that someone else, maybe a parent, set out for them. What matters is how meaningful *you* find the objective. By asking yourself why it is important, you gain clarity and true motivation for achieving your goal.

Such careful questioning can help you to eliminate some things that might not be important, and for those that truly are important you can get more specific about why that is the case. When you understand what truly is driving a passion, you will get better results from your efforts to reach your goals.

For example, let's say you have a goal of retiring with a few million dollars in the bank and your house paid off. Why is that important to you? Do you mainly want to live a comfortable lifestyle? Do you want to give a lot of money away? Do you want to leave money for your children? All of those? What is it exactly that you want to do? It is important to know, because the "why" can have a lot to do with the path you take in reaching that goal. The design of your financial plan and portfolio will depend on it.

Or let's say your goal is to get into better shape. Why? Do you want to look a certain way? Do you want to be an endurance athlete? Do you want to have more flexibility and fewer aches and pains? Each of those reasons calls for a very different training program. The same is true of finances: the "why" of your objective might dictate a different path.

MY MILLIONAIRE ACTION PLAN

—*Dave*

When I was twenty-four, I developed a plan to become at least a millionaire by retirement. At the time, I was advising seniors on Medicare supplement and long-term care insurance. I saw by their example that you could work for forty years and have little to show for it, perhaps nothing. That realization scared me. I began to put saving ahead of everything else in life. I made it my financial habit to save first, spend second. I figured out how much I needed to set aside every month to become a millionaire, and I saved that amount first before spending anything.

Let me share with you my action items as they were when I was twenty-four and as they are today, thirty-four years later.

At age twenty-four...

We were living with my mother-in-law and struggling after I experienced two business "learning experiences." In December 1982, I started in the insurance business with a wife and six-month-old child. My action items:

1. Plan to save enough to be at least a millionaire. Save first, spend what's left.

2. Get life insurance to protect my family if I were to die.

3. Set up a will and all documents needed to protect children if my wife and I both died.

4. Grow an emergency account equal to six months' income, save for a house.

5. Be the top agent in Arizona and build a renewal income for financial security.

At age fifty-eight...

As you can see, I have a lot more action items now, and they have changed over the decades:

1. As a business owner, five main items:

   - Set direction and vision to eliminate potential to be disrupted.

   - Have and update a succession plan to protect clients and employees.

   - Mentor David and all employees to be even more excellent in their roles.

   - Grow our value and positive impact on lives of clients, employee, and others.

   - Money will follow value creation.

2. Work with CPA to keep taxes as low as possible.

3. Keep personal budget moderate enough to save more than I send to the IRS.

4. Help children as appropriate, mostly guidance, but have them be self-sufficient.

5. Have trust avoid any potential estate, transfer costs, or other taxes, as possible.

6. Have trust protect Maryann, then Michelle (disabled), and rest of children and grandchildren in the event of any divorce, calamity, creditor, or predator.

7. We want to help our children and grandchildren know our values and why we did what we did, to avoid any inheritance trauma that could hurt them or cause division in family relationships.

8. Review annually how to optimize assets for potential retirement income, security income for Maryann, or transfer at our death.

9. Be parents and grandparents but strive to be good friends and the most trusted confidants our children or grandchildren could have, especially during their teen years.

10. Be joyful and grateful, and find joy and happiness in relationships and the beauty of life.

———— THINKING POINTS ————

1. What is your long-term guidepost that helps you keep all your decisions focused?

2. What is your action plan and priority list for this year? How do you learn from past experiences to improve your future?

3. What process do you have in place to prevent messes?

_____

CHAPTER 3

CHECKLISTS FOR SUCCESS

Commercial air travel is one of the safest ways to get around the world today, and yet nobody can deny that when something goes seriously wrong on a flight, the plane is likely to crash. The margin of error is slim. What makes flying so safe is the emphasis that airlines place on checklists and procedures.

The maintenance crews and the flight crews must regularly and thoroughly check and double check priority lists that simply must not be ignored. They cannot gloss over even routine matters. There are lists for scheduled maintenance, for preflight system checks, for the instructions by flight attendants, and for the pilots, both on the runway and in the air. There are takeoff procedures and landing procedures, all under the vigilance of air traffic controllers in the tower.

All of those checks are in accordance with a time frame and a specifically defined procedure and process. Experience has taught the airline industry and the regulators what must never be overlooked or ignored in order to avoid emergencies. And yet emergencies still happen from time to time—and when they do, there are checklists to handle those, as well. There is a proven system to produce the best outcome.

Just like with airline passenger safety, first you need a strategic plan and then a way to make sure your plan works. Checklists and procedures are the ongoing GPS toward your destination. They help you organize the complex, uncover new or hidden issues, and make sure your process and progress is consistent with your desired outcome.

In his book *The Checklist Manifesto*, Dr. Atul Gawande says surgeons, too, use checklists. "They provide a kind of cognitive net," he writes. "They catch mental flaws inherent in all of us, flaws of memory and attention and thoroughness. ... I have yet to get through a week in surgery without the checklist's leading us to catch something we would have missed."

For a pilot or surgeon, missing something important could be a matter of life or death. A serious lapse in your financial planning probably won't kill you, but you certainly could be in for a rough trip. To avoid that, you will need to be making a lot of systems checks: Are you on track for a reliable and lasting flow of income? Are you adjusting for conditions? Have you built in appropriate protections against risk? We develop and maintain these checklists for our clients.

QUESTIONS FOR SELECTING THE RIGHT ADVISOR

Is the financial advisor a fiduciary? (Is he/she legally obligated to act in your best interests?)

How is the advisor compensated?

Does that put the advisor on the same side of the table as you?

Does the advisor seem more like a salesperson?

Is there comprehensive advice, alignment, and synergy among all the areas of your financial life, or are things being done on a drive-by basis?

Does the advisor have access and experience in a broad range of solutions?

Is there a possibility the advisor's firm dictates or restricts what they can do?

Is there transparency on all fees, commissions, and incentives?

Did you ask the advisor, "Do you own it?" and, if not, "Why not?"

Listing and Reviewing Priorities

In the last chapter, we emphasized the importance of knowing where you are going in life and starting with the end in mind. You need to shrink the gap between where you are and where you want to go. So many obligations compete for your attention, and that is why it's wise to focus on your progress and not lose heart about how far you still must go. Each day, though, you will face decisions about what is most important, so you need a clear sense of priority.

A priority list is the first thing you should have when developing a plan, and in the last chapter we looked at how to identify those top goals. Every year we review each client's overall priorities. In that review, we consider whether any new priorities should move to the top of the list. Has anything emerged in life that might have moved ahead of the previous priorities?

We had a client who came to us because he was unhappy with his previous advisor. His wife had died, and he had set up a trust in her name. Under the terms, he could use the income from the trust, but it protected the assets so that they would go to his two sons when he died. He had no intention of remarrying—until he fell in love a few years later. We recommended a prenuptial agreement, drafted by a professional. The prenup sought to take care of the second wife without disturbing the original estate plan with his first wife. After seven years of marriage, our client's perspective changed: he told us he wanted to make more provisions for the second wife. Working with his attorney, he revised the estate plan. When he dies, his second wife will also be able to use the trust income for as long as she lives. Then the assets will pass on to the sons.

Situations and priorities certainly do change over time and in a great many ways. The markets rise and fall. You get a life-altering diagnosis. A loved one needs help right away. Someone gets married, someone dies. Good financial planning provides a framework in which we can know what needs to be done in such circumstances. A priority list updated annually will help you to respond proactively.

Nothing Overlooked

The checklist and priority list process also will help to ensure that you do not overlook something. When we begin working with new clients, quite often we find a few things that have been forgotten, misplaced, or ignored. When they come to us for help in solving some current issue, we typically discover during our conversation that some other issue also needs attention. A thorough overview, guided by a checklist, helps to uncover such areas of concern. One couple recently came in to talk about how to handle an inheritance. That prompted a discussion about their estate planning, and it turned out that they had not updated it in over twenty years.

We once worked with a couple who had a significant age differ-ence. Before they married, the husband had done a lot of investing. He had more than three hundred investments in an amazing array of things, sometimes buying just a share or two. The couple had some immediate and glaring problems. One was apparent because of their age difference: he was in his eighties and in failing health. They were unclear about the extent of the investments, most of which were in his name only. When he passed away, his wife would face the prospect of dealing with more than three hundred financial positions that would need paperwork, reconciliation, and perhaps legal documents to get them into her name and provide for her financial security.

Over a couple of years, they brought to us every piece of mail that came from a financial institution, and eventually we were able to assemble those investments into a revocable trust. They knew exactly what they had, and it was all gathered together in the trust and titled so that the wife would not face a nightmare upon his passing. The other problem that we solved for her was that when he did die, the cost basis of all those positions became their value at the date of his death, not what he had originally paid years earlier and did not have the records for. That automatic step-up was a big tax advantage that saved a lot of accounting work and got the paperwork down to one account instead of three hundred different ones.

All of that came about because of procedures and checklists. The checklists, along with questionnaires, help us to discover essential information and anticipate what could happen so that we can take the appropriate actions.

A Variety of Checklists

Busy people often just make their decisions as they go along. They don't think long term about how all the pieces will fit together. It's as if they are trying to assemble a jigsaw puzzle that has no picture, just plain cardboard on each side. If they could only see the overall design, they would have a much easier time of sliding those pieces into place.

That is what a prioritized checklist, like "My Millionaire Action Plan" discussed earlier, can do for you. You will know what's coming up. It's like that jigsaw puzzle: as you assemble the pieces, you can take pride in what you are doing, all the while referencing the big picture. Checklists help you see whether a decision you are considering will fit into your plan. For virtually anything you do that is repeatable, a checklist will set up the process for doing it better. It makes life easier, and it brings you better results.

Financial planning checklists can come in many forms. You might have a list designed to avoid forgetting important matters. You might have one to prompt thinking about the future and one for making financial decisions. You might have a checklist for choosing an advisor.

We work with our clients to get such things written down so that they can focus on accomplishing the steps toward their goals. Life happens, and emergencies arise. The unanticipated can change your course and threaten to wreck your plans. In developing your checklists, we can help you to make sure you cover all of the contingencies. We can help to identify issues that you might not have thought to bring into the picture.

It's all part of keeping you on track and holding you accountable to your goals. We have seen a wide range of issues and how they have played out for others, so we can help you to benefit from those lessons. We know what others have needed on their checklists, and that helps us to create the ones best suited for you.

The financial industry is complex, and it isn't getting any simpler. You can choose from a wide variety of products and strategies. That in itself makes a good case for checklists, which help you to approach your financial life systematically and practically. They clarify the complex. In simplicity is elegance. When your vision is clear, you can see so much more.

A CHECKLIST FOR FINANCIAL PLANNING

Checklists and questionnaires help to clarify your priorities and keep you on track toward your goals. Here's one on the broad issues of financial planning. How many of these items can you check off as ones that you have fully addressed?

- ✓ Alignment and synergy exist among all the areas of your financial life, and things are not being done on a drive-by basis.

- ✓ You are not listening to common persuasion tactics when making financial decisions.

- ✓ You are able to pinpoint where you are receiving unbiased financial advice from competent and trusted sources.

- ✓ If you are acting as your family's chief financial officer, you have put a plan in place for the things that make your financial house vulnerable.

- ✓ You have evaluated how difficult it would be for your spouse to take over the financial decision making.

- ✓ You have put a plan in place to make it easier for your spouse or survivors if you are not able to manage the details of your financial life.

- ✓ There are steps and systems that help in managing all the intricate details of your financial life.

✓ You are not allowing your financial life to become overly complex or chaotic because you are saying yes to too many opportunities and not saying no enough.

✓ You have increased your awareness of the cognitive fallacies that could influence you to make unwise financial decisions.

────────── T H I N K I N G   P O I N T S ──────────

1. Have you created a priority list for your life? If so, have you reviewed it recently?

2. Are you aware of all past investments and their impact on your portfolio?

CHAPTER 4

DON'T SHOOT YOURSELF IN THE FOOT

Would you intentionally shoot yourself in the foot? Can you imagine watching someone taking aim at their own foot in an effort to shoot themselves? And yet it can happen all the time with your finances. It is never intentional, though. Here is how it happens.

We have a cousin who was pheasant hunting one time and literally shot himself in the foot. He lost most of his big toe and put a nice hole in his boot. The boot was easier to repair than his toe, but how could he possibly shoot himself in the foot?

The only explanation we can think of is that he was thinking he was too experienced and smart to use all the safety rules at the time. He wanted to rest his arm and put down his gun, but he didn't want to put the gun on the ground, so he rested the end of the barrel on his boot.

When you are tired and cold from a day of hunting, it is easy to ignore some important rules of gun safety—namely, you must keep the safety switch on until you are ready to shoot; you don't put your finger inside the trigger guard until you're ready to shoot; and you never point the barrel at anything you don't want to hit. He had his finger inside the trigger guard with the safety off, and when he picked up the gun he accidentally lifted it by the trigger, hence the hole in his foot.

Our cousin made the mental mistake of taking shortcuts with the tried-and-true gun safety rules that could have prevented his injury, and, maybe more importantly, his embarrassment. Investors often shoot themselves in the foot as well, by making mental mistakes or taking mental shortcuts in their finances.

The journey will be easier if you are not limping because you hurt yourself. We'll discuss strategies to avoid the three most-common areas of self-inflicted injury:

1. How to avoid mental shortcuts that can slow you down

2. How to avoid the mind-set that wrecks results

3. How to eliminate excruciating decisions by making the right small decisions

Mental Shortcuts

We could write volumes about the mental shortcuts that people take that hurt their returns or hinder their progress toward their goals. We'll examine a few of those in this chapter. Let's start with the most common and fundamental shortcut: considering only the surface-level information.

Think about an iceberg. About 10 percent of it is visible above the surface of the water. The remaining 90 percent of the iceberg is below the surface, where it is not easy to see. Sometimes, investors and other consumers of financial services only look at the 10 percent above the surface. They don't make the extra effort to look below the surface for what they need to know in order to make the better decisions that typically lead to better outcomes.

If you only look at the surface-level information, and if you ignore safety measures, you are bound to get in trouble. What you don't know, and what you don't do, can certainly hurt you. Our cousin probably could vouch for that. The captain of the *Titanic* might have had something to say about that, too, before he went down with the ship.

A FRUSTRATED COLUMNIST

—Dave

I once wrote a financial advice column for a monthly newspaper for seniors here in Arizona. I found that the hardest part of sitting down to put those words together every month was that I really did not know whom I was addressing in the column. Knowing that the audience was primarily of retirement age, or approaching it, gave me some sense of what to say, but it felt as if I had so many blanks that needed to be filled in.

As an investment advisor, I would much rather know about a person's entire situation so that I can give the best advice. Writing for that newspaper, I did not know whether the reader would be person A, person B, or person C, each of whom would have an entirely different personal scenario, so what I wrote tended to sound generic. There are many "what ifs" that need to be addressed in every individual case. Good advice for one person might be questionable or worse for another.

Nonetheless, many people get their advice from the media—whether through traditional publications and broadcasts or through the "new media" of online sources. Sometimes they even feel that because the information is free, they can save money by getting it there. It's an illusion. It's another of those mental shortcuts that bypass the hard work necessary to draft an individual financial plan.

Looking Below the Surface

In search of investment advice, many people do little more than scan the headlines, skim through financial magazines, turn up the volume now and then on a business news broadcast, or surf the Internet, primarily reassuring themselves of what they already believe to be true. They may even go to workshops to collect investment tips. What they find tends to be advice of a generic nature or skewed toward the promotion of a product. What they seldom find is information that gets below the surface.

Often people will fall back on some old axiom that they have accepted as gospel. The trouble is, it might not apply to their particular situation. For example, some people hold on to this quote from Warren Buffett on how long to keep an investment: "Our favorite holding period is forever." For one thing, he was referring to securities in "outstanding businesses with outstanding managements," which is a part of the quote that tends to get missed. And the typical investor is not Warren Buffett. He's not depending on any particular investment for his living expenses. And yet people will trot out his quote to rationalize a buy-and-hold mentality that might not be appropriate for them. They are letting a mental shortcut get in the way of analyzing their own situation.

In fact, just invoking the name of Warren Buffett, or others who are considered investment gurus, is a shortcut in itself. Sometimes investors believe that the best route to success is to simply mimic the experts. Unfortunately, research has shown that gurus are right only about half the time. That bit of below-the-surface information should convince investors of the importance of getting personalized advice, not pronouncements from some mountaintop.

Maybe you have seen checklists on how to choose a good advisor. Most of those checklists suggest that you consider the person's experience, education, licensing, certification, etc. They tell you to find out how the advisor is paid, whether by commission or fee or both. And that information, of course, is very important. But the checklists never seem to suggest that you find out about some below-the-surface information that we believe you need to know. A good line of questioning for a prospective advisor is this: "Do you own this investment yourself? How much and for how long? If I take your advice, how much will you get paid and when?"

Another mental shortcut is blind allegiance to the oft-touted principle that market timing never works. First of all, most information sources consider risk management and protection strategies as market timing and give it a negative connotation—they argue that if you miss the ten best days, you give up half your return. As mentioned in the book's introduction, risk management is when you try to protect against stock market losses when markets are declining. Many investors neglect to do any portfolio and risk management because they figure that they would just be engaging in some pointless exercise of trying to time the market. But what if this "fact" has been perpetuated simply because it meets an industry's income and profit goals and not your own? Remember that mutual fund managers are paid to manage stocks or other investments in their market segment.

They try to keep up with a benchmark and typically cannot invest outside of their particular market segment. Is it any surprise that big mutual fund companies tell us to buy, hold, and never sell?

Non-mutual fund professional managers may tell you that managing risk is essential for getting good returns. In other words, to preserve against loss, you have to do something. If you are to buy low and sell high—which most will agree is how to make money— you need to take action. Yes, trying to time the market based on surface information and emotion usually fails, but does that mean you should never adjust, manage risk, or balance your portfolio?

Those are a few examples of the mental shortcuts to avoid as you get beneath the surface. It takes some work, but you will find it to be well worth your time as your portfolio grows.

An Emotional Mess—Or a Mind-Set Change

Emotions get in the way of good investment decision making, period. And when it comes to investments, it is important to set emotions completely aside. When investors let fear and greed get involved, for example, they almost always do worse. There's two very common situations that we run across all the time that are examples of investors letting their emotions get the better of them. Think of them as opposite sides of the same coin.

On one end of the emotional spectrum, investors often sell their winners too soon and hold on to their losers too long. They do this because their human nature wants the positive emotional charge of "being right," which they get by locking in the gain of selling a winner. And what they don't want is the negative emotional charge of being wrong, which they would get if they sold their losers. The thing is, the number-one thing interested investors could do to increase their returns is to let their winners run longer and sell their losers sooner. For more on this, we highly recommend Daniel Kahneman's book *Thinking, Fast and Slow*. Considered the father of behavioral economics and winner of the Noble Prize in Economics, he offers much evidence in support of this idea.

On the other end of the emotional spectrum is the opposite mistake, which we usually see happen after a protracted run up or down in something that's making big headlines. Think tech stocks in 1999, real estate in 2007, and gold in 2011. A fundamental principle of wise investing is to buy low and sell high, and yet many people do exactly the opposite after they've already missed the boat. This emotional tendency drives investors to chase returns by purging a portfolio of investments that are doing poorly and buying more of the investments that have been doing awesome for a long time. They pay a premium for securities that are at their peak and at the same time overlook both bargains and risks in the marketplace. That's not the way to make money.

People do that nonetheless, because they want something that is causing them pain to just go away. They want to hitch their cart to something that seems able to ease their pain. Thus they buy high and sell low. In trying to manage their pain, they get more of it.

"It's not supposed to be easy," observed Charlie Munger, vice president of Berkshire Hathaway and Warren Buffett's right-hand man. "Anyone who finds it easy is stupid." It's a blunt but accurate assessment of the folly of taking shortcuts.

Our human nature can hurt returns. People's default behavior is not compatible with wise investing. In our experience, many people are aware, at least, that they are capable of succumbing to their own weakness. Whenever we ask groups of investors whether they ever have sold low and bought high, everyone concedes that they have made that mistake at some point.

A money manager at an investment conference that we attended said that he used a computer program to tell him what to buy and sell, and he would just implement the trades. The aim was to make decisions based on logic and math, not on emotions. At times he found that hard to do, considering what he was hearing on the news. "Sometimes I want to go into the bathroom and throw up when I have to implement what the investment strategy is telling me to do," he said.

If it is hard for professional money managers to keep the emotions at bay, you can imagine that for the average investor it can be nearly impossible. Warren Buffett has said he likes to buy companies when they are on the operating table—that is, when they are sick and are priced low because of it. Most individual investors would not invest that way. Their emotions block opportunities. "Individuals who cannot master their emotions," observed Benjamin Graham, a mentor to Buffett and to many other investing legends, "are ill-suited to profit from the investment process."

Investor Biases

We see the world through a variety of lenses, and not all of them give us clearer vision. Now, let's take a look at some of those mental shortcuts in the context of investment decision making. Here are just a few of the emotional pitfalls or biases that have been identified as having the potential to lead investors astray.

> *Recency bias:* Investors tend to believe that what they recently have experienced will continue. They tend to keep fighting the last war. After the market has crashed, they steer clear of it for fear that it will crash again. On the flip side, once the market has been rising for three or four years, they tend to invest as if it will

never go back down. Market strategists regularly issue recommendations on how much of a portfolio should be devoted to stocks, bonds, and cash. At the turn of the millennium, when the dot-com bubble was at its peak, strategists tended to recommend a higher stock weighting. Several years later, in the depths of the recession, such recommendations were far fewer.

Choice paralysis: People tend to think that the more choices they have, the more likely they will be to make a wise decision. Instead, they may feel discouraged from making any decision at all. Overloaded with information, they cannot make up their minds. Paralyzed by uncertainty, investors may end up doing nothing, thereby suffering losses—or lost opportunities. Research has suggested, for example, that a 401(k) retirement plan that offers a wide variety of selections on the investment menu is not necessarily in the best interests of either the employees or the company.

The herd instinct: When everyone is running with a thriving bull market upward, individual investors tend to follow—as they also do when everyone is running from the downturning bear market. The herd instinct is what can lead to big rallies or sell-offs in the market that do not seem to be based on underlying conditions. Institutions can tend to follow the herd, as well. The investments that one chooses often reflect the investments that others are choosing.

Confirmation bias: People tend to seek information that confirms what they believe, ignoring what doesn't fit in with those beliefs. They look for facts and opinions to support the conclusion they have already come to. Their preconceived notions get in the way of good decision making. That is often the case for investors.

They may dump their stock in a company based on news stories that it is failing, overlooking a glowing report of an exciting new initiative. They sell at a low—and could very well miss the party. The solution? Seek out a balanced assortment of information and opinions.

These are human tendencies. What is important is to understand that you are heir to them so that you can appropriately deal with them. Whenever your predispositions influence your decisions, you may not be exploring everything you need to know, and your investments could suffer. Once again, it comes down to keeping emotions out of the equation. Emotions are great for poetry but not for portfolios.

Your overall worldview or mind-set, too, can greatly affect your ability to make wise investment decisions. If you are pessimistic about where the country and the world are heading, your investment decisions are likely to be very risk averse—and that can backfire on you. If you are overly optimistic about the future, you are liable to take too much risk and fail to pull back appropriately if the economy and markets get rough. You will be much better off if you take a neutral stance and base your investments on how well a particular strategy will advance you toward your life goals. Leave pessimism and optimism out of it.

Crystal balls are for the mystics. Nobody can predict the future. Still, you will find plenty of financial prognosticators out there. They do get it right sometimes, but they could also get it right sometimes by flipping a coin. The best you can do is to measure the probabilities, favor the decisions that will give you the best chances for success, and adjust course when necessary.

A Disciplined Strategy

You need a strong, written investment strategy so that you can strive confidently toward clear goals and not end up limping in the forest like our cousin. When you lack specific guidelines, you risk letting emotions and shortsighted desires control your investment decisions. You need rules to follow, and you need to follow those rules.

As we think about our cousin's misfortune, here are just three such rules for investors that come to mind:

1. Use the safety switch until you are ready to shoot. Always think about the risk and a potential risk management strategy before you jump in.

2. Keep your fingers off the trigger until it's time to fire. Always explore the trade-offs between the option in your sights and another option, or several.

3. Don't point the barrel at anything you don't want to hit. That's how investment accidents happen. Ask yourself, is this a good time to do this or am I acting out of emotion?

Once you have committed to an investment strategy, you should write down those rules. A written plan makes you more accountable to what you have set out to accomplish. It gives you a rational, long-range view, based on sound and timeless investment principles that keep you on track toward your goals. It will help you to avoid rash decisions in the heat of the moment.

This is how small decisions—made when there is no pressure about how you are going to follow the investment discipline in your comprehensive plan—can save you from excruciating ones later. For example, if you have a strategy of risk management to prevent large losses in a position or in your portfolio, and you follow that discipline, you have moved toward eliminating tough, emotional decisions when markets get roughest. And we believe if you can avoid those extreme emotions you have a much better chance of taking advantage of opportunities as they arise.

You no doubt live by an ethical or moral code and weigh your decisions by it rather than reacting from the gut whenever an issue arises. It makes sense to have a code for your financial life as well, because gut reactions can destroy a portfolio. Today's markets are more challenging than ever, with a wide range of products that often come with high fees and commissions. A disciplined planning process may help you to reassess your positions, cutting out weak ones and looking for strong potential, all the while managing the risks.

That calls for professional guidance. To do it well, you need experience, training, and specialized knowledge. Most people will need to partner up and consult with someone who has the expertise to develop that comprehensive plan. You need to work with someone you can trust to help you look below the surface, building a portfolio of investments that will serve you well for the long term, not just ones that look good at the moment.

A good advisor will help you develop a disciplined strategy and keep you accountable to it. Somebody should be at your side to remind you to flip on the safety switch when you are at risk of shooting yourself in the foot.

TAMING THOSE EMOTIONS

—David

In choosing an investment recently, I took three steps that could help you in your own decisions. Emotions are powerful. Greed and fear can subconsciously lead investors to buy or sell at the wrong time. Here is how I kept my emotions in check as I made an intentional invest-ment choice:

Step one: Ask the right questions, both the pros and the cons.

Step two: If you choose to make the investment, document your answers to those questions. Write them down, type them out, whatever you need to do so that you can refer to them later.

Step three: When you want to change out of this invest-ment, either out of frustration (fear) or because you think you found something better (greed), refer back to your written answers to the pros and cons. This will serve as a double check on your emotions.

The key is to ask the right questions. First I looked at the pros:

- Why do I think this investment is a good fit, given my overall financial program?

- Why do I like this investment?

- In what sort of market environment will this invest-ment do well?

- What is the benefit of this investment versus all the other options out there?

- Is this a phenomenal opportunity or just a distraction to which I should say "no"?

Also, these are great questions to ask your advisor about anything they recommend.

The pros are easy to identify, and in today's sales-driven culture they are usually the only thing you see. I documented my answers so that if I saw another compelling opportunity I would have a good way to compare so that I don't chase some shiny object. I also think that documenting those answers gives me the fortitude to stick with this investment even when it struggles. I believe that's what will give me the best chance to avoid distractions and find long-term success.

I then looked at the cons:

- What problems does it have?

- What have been the worst losses in this investment or a similar one, from the high-water mark to the absolute bottom, historically?

- When has this kind of investment really struggled in the past and why?

- In what sort of market environment will this investment do poorly?

- Can I identify any time periods where I would really be frustrated with the results for this kind of investment?[4]

---

4   As an investor, when you're presented with information or researching how an investment has done in the past, the data is usually presented in calendar years. In other words, you might see how something did in 2008, 2009, 2010, etc. But—and this is huge—evaluating past performance that way can hide a lot of valuable information, which is what this question is getting at. For example, say you're looking at an investment and in 2013 you see it made 3 percent. But what if you found out that during 2013, it dropped 65 percent in a couple of months but then was able to make that back and then a little more before the end of the year? Knowing that gives you a much better perspective than just knowing that something made x percent in a given calendar year.

- Will I be able to stomach this investment through its worst times (so that I'll still be there for all the good times)?

Again, these are great questions to ask your advisor about anything they recommend.

By answering these questions and documenting my answers, I did a couple of things. First I determined my risk exposure and how much I could lose. I got real about when, and in which environments, this investment would put my stomach in knots. I took off the rose-colored glasses. By taking a hard look at the negatives, I got outside my emotions and what I thought I knew about the investment and really shined a mental spotlight on things I might not have otherwise considered.

In the end I decided the investment was a good choice—but it soon was losing money, even as the overall market was doing okay. You can imagine how I felt! I could have done much better in the general market. How frustrated would you be?

Had I not asked the questions and documented the answers, I might have decided to pull the plug. Instead I reviewed my answers, particularly those related to the cons, to see whether I was experiencing anything historically abnormal for this investment based on my initial research. I concluded that I wasn't. By reviewing my answers, I was able to keep my emotions in check and stick with my decision, which since has turned out to be the right move. I avoided shooting myself in the foot.

———————— T H I N K I N G   P O I N T S ————————

1. What is your overall investment and risk management strategy?

2. What are your action steps/points in rising markets and declining markets?

3. What other questions should you be asking now, when extreme emotions aren't involved?

CHAPTER 5

SOLVING THE PORTFOLIO DILEMMA

"Most people spend more time and energy going around problems than in trying to solve them."

—Henry Ford, automaker

Here is the dilemma: to invest for growth, you want to invest in something that goes up, but it also has the chance of going down—way down. Everyone is happy when it goes up, and almost any plan works. A rising tide lifts all boats. Hardly anyone though has a plan for when an investment or market goes down and how to manage the potential for losses—loss of money, loss of time, and loss of confidence.

Almost everyone advises you to *follow a trend*. And the trend they tell you to follow is usually a 116-year chart of the stock market going up, and those times when it goes down look pretty small on a long chart. We, too, believe you should follow a trend; however, we know you do not have 116 years, or in many cases even 20 years, to wait for things to work out if something goes wrong.

DOW JONES INDUSTRIAL AVERAGE (DJIA)

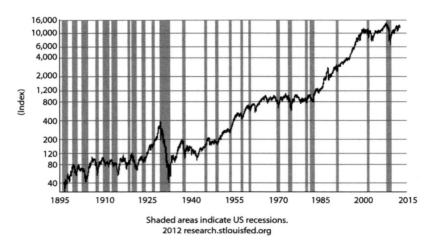

Shaded areas indicate US recessions.
2012 research.stlouisfed.org

Source: Dow Jones & Company

Sometimes Wall Street financial firms provide news and information with a positive slant, regardless of what is happening in the market. You will hear that it will get better and that there is never a bad time to invest. Some of them will tell you that you should ride out the ups and downs because that is the only way to get good long-term results. They get paid when you invest and stay invested, so they will tell you that there is never a reason to sell. But is it a myth or reality?

In the sixteen years from March 24, 2000, until March 24, 2016, the stock market (as represented by the S&P 500 Cap Weighted Index) increased in price only 32 percent. During that period, it first lost 49 percent of its value from March 2000 until October 2002 and took 87 months to get back to where it had been in March 2000. Later, from October 2007 until March 2009, it lost 56 percent of its value and took 66 months to get back where it was in October

2007.[5] Despite that emotional roller coaster, what is the advice that is the most common today? "Stay on the ride; everything's going to be okay." Will it be okay for you? It could depend on when you need the money.

BEAR MARKET FACTS

- Bear markets are defined as a 20 percent decline or greater in the S&P 500 Index.

- Since 1929 sixteen bear markets have occurred.

- Average frequency of a new bear market since 1929: every 4.8 years.

- Average depth of a bear market: 38.24 percent decline.

- Average duration of a bear market: seventeen months.

- Average time lost making up a bear market loss: sixty months.

- In fifty-two of eighty-six years (60 percent of the time), people have been putting their own money back in their pocket. All new growth occurred during just 40 percent of the time period.

*Source: www.standardandpoors.com

**The Standard and Poor's Stock Index (S&P 500) is an unmanaged representative of the US stock market, without regard for company size and cannot be invested in directly.

---

5   Standard & Poor's, www.standardandpoors.com.

S&P 500 Corrections

September 1929 through March 2016 (86 years)

BEAR MARKET	DURATION	DECLINE	TIME TO BREAK EVEN
1. September 1929–June 1932	33 months	−86.7%	302 months
2. July 1933–March 1935	20 months	−33.9%	28 months
3. March 1937–March 1938	12 months	−54.5%	107 months
4. November 1938–April 1942	41 months	−45.8%	77 months
5. May 1946–March 1948	22 months	−28.1%	49 months
6. August 1956–October 1957	14 months	−21.6%	25 months
7. December 1961–June 1962	6 months	−28.0%	22 months
8. February 1966–October 1966	8 months	−22.2%	16 months
9. November 1968–May 1970	18 months	−36.1%	39 months
10. January 1973–October 1974	21 months	−48.2%	91 months
11. November 1980–August 1982	21 months	−27.1%	25 months
12. August 1987–December 1987	3 months	−33.5%	23 months
13. July 1990–October 1990	3 months	−19.9%	7 months
14. July 1998–October 1998	3 months	−21.2%	3 months
15. March 2000–October 2002	31 months	−49.1%	**87 months**
16. October 2007–March 2009	17 months	−56.78%	**66 months**

Source: www.standardandpoors.com

Jack Bogle, founder and chairman of mutual fund giant Vanguard Group, is widely credited for popularizing index funds, a staple for buy-and-hold investors. In a recent CNBC interview, Bogle startled the commentators by telling them to "prepare for at least two declines of 25–30 percent, maybe even 50 percent, in the coming decade."

For a buy-and-hold guy, that's a shocking scenario, isn't it? Bogle said it was shocking, but not worrisome, because the market has never failed to recover from one of those 50 percent declines. He went through one from 1973 to 1974, another from 2001 to 2003, and another from 2008 to 2009. He said the only way to invest is to hang on through the cycle; trying to guess when it's going to go way up or way down is simply not a productive way to put your money to work.[6]

Buy-and-hold is a valid approach that a lot of investment strategies are based on. You just have to ask yourself, *is that what you want?* What that philosophy says is, to be a smart investor, you have to emotionally adapt to the market and hang on through gut-wrenching times.

We suggest a different approach one with a disciplined process with simple rules to follow that can help you avoid the gut wrenching emotional choices that can lead to large losses. You should think about using a strategy where your investments—not your emotions—adapt to market conditions. We don't believe this is all you should do, but we do believe it should be central to your investing approach. But before we tell you our approach, let us give you an analogy to illustrate how most people get it wrong.

What does a farmer know that investors don't? They know to plant in the spring and to harvest in the fall. If you think about the four seasons, you can better understand almost everything about the economy, the stock market, different sectors and securities, and a variety of investment opportunities.

In the springtime, we see small shoots emerging through the ground—much as a stock, industry sector, market, or economy starts to move upward after a downturn. If that initial growth takes hold, then the summer comes along and can spark a strong growing season. As the stock, industry sector, market, or economy gains momentum, investors, businesses, and workers can begin to believe the season will never end. Then comes fall, when growth slows or contracts. A

---

6   Matthew Boesler, "JACK BOGLE WARNS: Prepare For Two Massive Market Declines In The Next Decade," Business Insider, April 1, 2013, http://www.businessinsider.com/jack-bogle-warns-of-two-50-percent-market-declines-in-next-10-years-2013-4.

business may start to decline, taking its stock price with it. It could be one company, an industry sector, the whole market, or the economy. In winter, if it gets severe and the downturn accelerates, you could lose value in your investments, your business, or your job. At this emotional depth, it's hard to imagine spring again and recognize those first small shoots of growth.

A stock, industry sector, market or economy will go through these four seasons and could start over again. (A single company stock could go bankrupt though and not start the cycle again). Individual companies, different industry sectors or markets could/will be going thru the seasons at different paces and times. For example the energy sector could be in the dead of winter while the health care sector is enjoying summer.

CYCLE OF INVESTOR EMOTIONS

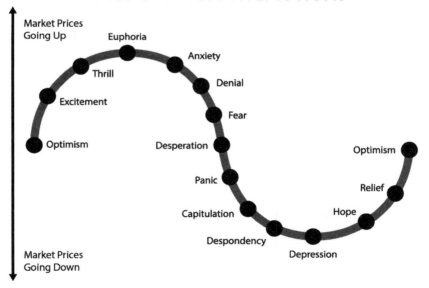

So what is that one thing you can do to deal effectively with the swing of the economic seasons? How can you overcome those emotions? You just need a different mind-set on how you view those seasons. Rather than believing that this summer is different and will never end, you need a clear understanding that the markets, economies, or investments do go up and down, and you need a plan for dealing with that reality. Isn't that far better than just hoping it isn't so?

What does a farmer do when the crops are ready to be picked? Does he leave them in the field, thinking they have to go through all four seasons if he is to get a good long-term yield? The farmer understands the importance of pruning a tree to get more fruit in the fall, and he knows when it's time for the harvest. And that's the kind of harvest mentality that can help investors avoid those winter losses.

What do we mean by harvesting? Harvesting means pruning a weakening investment position, changing to a stronger one, or selling to preserve capital. Harvesting doesn't ignore the fact that markets can go down and you can lose money. It doesn't accept as a fact of life that you have to ride out big losses to attain the market's average returns. It's a simple discipline of striving to buy in the spring and sell in the fall.

Like a smart farmer, you need to be intentional about what you plant in the spring, grow during the summer, harvest in the fall, and protect and evaluate during the winter. Each investment season follows the previous in sequence, just not in nature's regular annual rhythm. After winter comes spring, although if you've had big losses it can be hard to see when it starts. Summer gives way to fall and then winter again. It's been that way every time so far in the history of the markets.

EMOTIONAL CYCLE WORKS AGAINST YOU

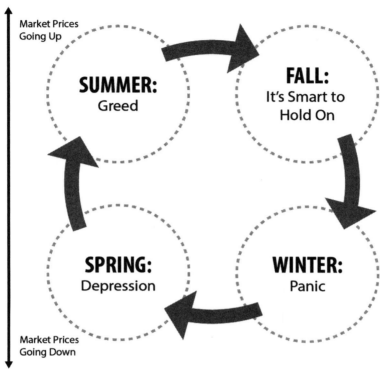

Oftentimes, investors go through this cycle of emotions where you hang on without harvesting, panic when things get too bad, sell out at the bottom, get too depressed to recognize the spring, don't invest again until late in the cycle, and then get greedy when the market is doing well. Worst of all, you can feel unconfident and unsure about what to do next.

It is essentially an undisputed fact in the financial industry that investors buy more at the top of market cycles and sell more at the bottom. Research finds investors lose about up to half, depending on time period reviewed, of their potential return going through this cycle by buying high and selling low.[7]

The most basic rule of investing is to buy low and sell high, but the emotional cycle and the idea that you hang on no matter what, in

---

7   DALBAR's Quantitative Analysis of Investor Behavior Period ending Dec. 31, 2016.

other words, you don't sell high, changes what should be like a farmer's cycle into an emotional cycle helping many to take the wrong action.

Because of this emotional roller coaster, most firms will recommend an "all-weather" portfolio that you will hold long term because it has been "optimized" based on past history. They may rebalance it from time to time, but it is well diversified across many asset classes all the time, and the idea is that you stay with it through all market conditions. But will the future be like the past several years that the portfolio is optimized for? Interest rates, for example, have generally declined for about thirty-four years now, and declining rates generally help bond investment returns and stock prices to rise. What if interest rates just stop declining or go up?

In the 1980s with a roughly 200 percent gain and the 1990s with over a 300 percent gain, the more stocks you owned the better. It was completely different in the next decade, 2000 to 2009, with roughly a 20 percent loss in the S&P 500 Index.[8]

Another factor is that when you diversify into almost every asset class, you are going to have some that are detracting from your returns.

Maybe instead of buying and holding a broad array of asset classes and holding them forever, you could still be diversified but instead concentrate on asset classes that are starting their spring and summer cycles of growth/strength, and harvest or trim those that are starting their fall/weakness cycles and avoid the winter that could happen there. As you further examine why it is important to recognize the investment seasons, it is important to understand two things:

- What can you measure to see the seasons change?

- What makes you money?

---

8   Crestmontresearch.com

AN INTENTIONAL DISCIPLINED PROCESS

Market Prices
Going Up

SUMMER:
Hold

FALL:
Harvest

SPRING:
Buy

WINTER:
Evaluate

Market Prices
Going Down

You might do better with an intentional, disciplined process, where you want to buy in the spring, hold during the summer, harvest in the fall, and evaluate or preserve in winter.

Think about your investments: In the simplest form, what makes prices go up and down? Just as supply and demand determines the prices at the grocery store, likewise when more people want to buy a particular investment than want to sell it, the price will rise to a point where others will also sell. When fewer people want to buy it than sell it, the price will almost always go down, regardless of the underlying fundamentals of the investment.

You may recall the Beanie Babies craze. What were they worth before everybody had to have one? Five dollars. What were they worth at the peak of their popularity? Hundreds and projected to be thousands. What were they worth when that extra demand went away? Three for ten dollars. The Beanie Babies didn't change. What changed was the number of people who were buying them and selling them—and that had a lot to do with how much talk about them was circulating. Media hype helps drive up prices. There's a lesson there: when it comes to investments, what is in the news can lead people to invest poorly.

Howard Marks, cofounder of Oaktree Capital Management, is known among investors for his "Oaktree memos" to clients on economic insights and investment strategies. In his memo of March 18, 2008, he described the three stages of a bull market that he learned forty years ago.[9] This is what he wrote:

- The first, when a few forward-looking people begin to believe things will get better.

- The second, when most investors realize improvement is actually underway.

- The third, when everyone's sure things will get better forever.

ANATOMY OF A TREND AND NEWS CYCLE
PRICE OF INVESTMENT TIMELINE

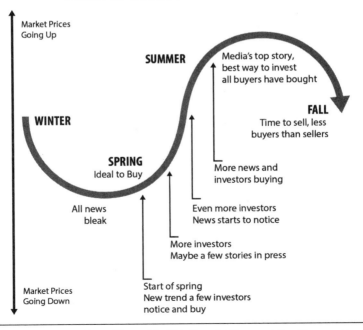

---

9   Howard Marks, to Oaktree Clients, "The Tide Goes Out," memo, https://www.oaktreecapi-tal.com/docs/default-source/memos/2008-03-18-the-tide-goes-out.pdf?sfvrsn=2.

Conversely, this is how Marks described the three stages of a bear market in his memo:

- The first, when just a few prudent investors recognize that, despite the prevailing bullishness, things won't always be rosy.

- The second, when most investors recognize things are deteriorating.

- The third, when everyone's convinced things can only get worse.

ANATOMY OF A TREND AND NEWS CYCLE
PRICE OF INVESTMENT TIMELINE

How can you measure supply and demand for an investment? By measuring the price movements. When were Beanie Babies most in demand and media coverage the highest? When prices were the highest.

That answers the question about what you can measure. You measure supply and demand by price movement. Using Marks's description and the visual examples of how media coverage amplifies interest, popularity, and the human emotions of fear and greed, you can clearly see the cycle of spring, summer, fall, and winter.

Now for the second question: What makes you money? You make money either from the income from the investment or from the increase in its value. So ideally you are looking for investments that are on an uptrend, where more people are buyers than sellers, and conversely you want to know when supply exceeds demand and prices start declining. Even if you buy an investment for income, in some cases the value can drop more than the income you thought you would receive. The price you pay to buy and the price you get when you sell always matter.

BIG PICTURE CONCEPTS:
WHAT IS "TREND FOLLOWING"?

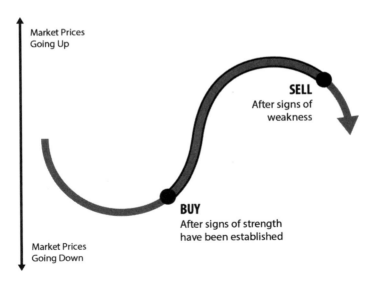

Market Prices
Going Up

SELL
After signs of
weakness

BUY
After signs of strength
have been established

Market Prices
Going Down

We believe in a disciplined process for selling when an investment becomes unfavored and supply exceeds demand. The downturn could be mild and the price might go back up, in which case you could invest there again. But in a severe downturn or weakness, you can save yourself a lot of money, emotional pain, and time trying to recover that loss later. The worst part is continuing to lose money and still not knowing what to do, when emotions can easily overtake you.

Is a disciplined risk management strategy market timing? Market timing is defined as making adjustments based on what you think is going to happen. Many times people think with their emotions because of the news, fear, or greed. That's not good. In contrast, managing risk using trend following involves observing what is actually happening based on one of the most powerful forces on earth—supply and demand.

Another concept to understand is that one investment or market could be entering its fall, potentially soon to be winter, while another investment or market could be just starting its spring. In that case, we use what's called trend adaptation.

WHAT DOES "TREND ADAPTATION" LOOK LIKE?

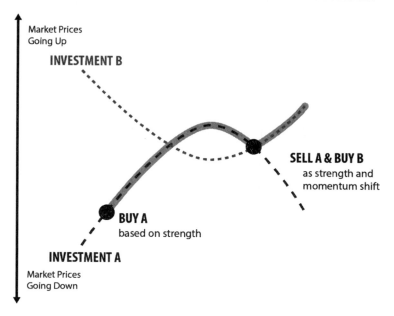

Of course, not all stocks are operating on the same "seasonal schedule." Working with a professional who uses a math-based, logic-based investment system may save you a lot of headaches and possibly millions—we believe you can do much better, with less stress, with a math-based investment process that keeps the emotions out of your investment decisions. The key is to find investments in their spring and in their fall. We call our process Risk-Adjusting Portfolios™. These are portfolios that strive to do three things:

- buy when strength rises

- hold if still strong

- sell when asset weakens

Risk-Adjusting Portfolios™

We have heard it said that a house must be built three times before it is complete: first, in our minds; second, as a blueprint; and third, the actual construction. It's the same with our financial lives.

The financial plan should come first, and the investments should be chosen to fit in with it and with your unique circumstances. You likely will become unhappy with an investment style that is chosen at random when it does not advance your overall goals.

Therefore, you need to consider a variety of variables, including how much risk you can tolerate under the circumstances. For instance, perhaps you and your spouse have a generous pension and therefore much less need for guaranteed investments. With part of your portfolio, you may be able to accept greater risk with the potential for greater return. That is just one example to illustrate the importance of grasping the overall financial picture before deciding how to invest.

In general, we have found that a successful investment process requires a long-term time horizon of three years or more and must have the flexibility to include a diversity of strategies and styles—so you can change with the seasons but also have multiple ways to take advantage of each season. You would not focus on just a single summer growth strategy or just one winter safety strategy. In addition, your investment process should be in writing, and it must be based on a disciplined procedure, removed from emotion.

In addition, we recommend that investments be kept liquid and easily accessible whenever possible. Try to avoid an up-front load or back-end load or some period of time when you need to stay in an investment. You want to be able to make a change whenever you need to do so. Look for transparency in your investments and in the fees that you pay, and work with fiduciaries whose duty is to act in your best interests, not their own. You should know, to the penny, how much money you are paying for your investment advice. Always make sure that your advisor places your money with a third-party custodian and that your money is not commingled with other clients' money. This will help protect yourself and your wealth.

With those fundamentals in mind, you could take many approaches to your investments, depending on your circumstances, risk tolerance, and the economic season. With all those factors to consider, how can you know what will be best for you?

Let's look at research that shows us what factors help us make better investment returns over time.

THE PREMIER ANOMALIES

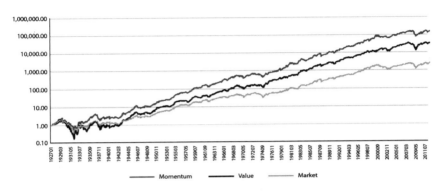

All performance numbers are based on the performance of non-investable indexes. Investors cannot invest directly in an index. Indexes have no fees. Examples presented on this slide are for illustrative purposes only and do not represent past or present recommendations. Past performance is not indicative of future results. Potential for profits is accompanied by possibility of loss. The relative strength strategy is NOT a guarantee. There may be times where all investments and strategies are unfavorable and depreciate in value.

PERCENT OF 36-MONTH ROLLING PERIODS WHERE FACTOR PORTFOLIO UNDERPERFORMED THE BROAD MARKET

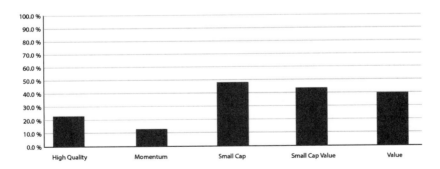

Our Risk-Adjusting Portfolios™ investment process is based on integrating three principles to ensure that you are investing in the right season and protected in the winter.

Relative strength/momentum is one of the main tools of our process. It is one way to measure and determine momentum. It is a framework for identifying the right investment season, as well as the strongest investments within that season. The concept is somewhat self-explanatory, in that you are assessing the strength of one investment as compared to others—stocks versus bonds, for example. You are looking for which is stronger at the moment, and then you look for what is strongest within the broad areas. For example, if US stocks are the strongest broad asset class, what are the strongest areas or sectors within US stocks? Because relative strength tends to persist—objects in motion tend to stay in motion—the momentum can help to keep you invested in stronger areas.

Value investing is another element of our approach that should be represented in a portfolio. In essence, value investing means buying what is on sale—what is selling below its "true" value. You are looking for the greatest opportunity to buy at a low price and sell later at a higher price when other investors see the true value. Value investing is, of course, a seasonal style and often most appropriate for the economic springtime of new growth. You might think of value investing as ballast for your portfolio. As in a boat, extra weight provides stability in rough waters. Meanwhile, relative strength and momentum are the motor. In times when the relative strength strategy is underperforming, the value investing strategy tends to outperform. Together, they work to produce an effective approach to managing your portfolio.

A *plan to harvest* is a third essential element of Risk-Adjusting Portfolios™. You need an action plan for your investments when the bad weather comes, as it surely will. When it does, you will need to harvest and preserve your gains and principle. No, you won't be making as much progress, and you may lose out on some opportunity—but you will lower your chances of losing a large part of your resources and having to change your lifestyle.

Together, those three components of our process add up to more than risk management. We think it's stress management. When your portfolio gets out of sorts, you can get out of sorts, too. Not knowing what to do can be frightening. When you create a financial plan, it can help work toward reducing your stress and enhancing your lifestyle. The small disciplines of the four seasons could save you from large gut-wrenching decisions later. Even when the markets are not behaving as you would like, you can know that your prudent oversight of your assets is under control. You have that plan in place.

Perhaps you have experienced a time when your portfolio lost a significant amount of its value. No doubt you felt pain and stress—those plunges can trigger emotions that often lead to bad decisions. Our process seeks to set that aside so that our clients need not feel such extreme levels of stress ever again.

We once met with a husband and wife who had reacted in separate ways with their separate investments to the economic downturn several years ago. The husband had gotten out of the market near its peak and gone to cash in 2007, before the crash. He never got back in. With her investments, the wife rode the market all the way down and all the way back up. The wife told us that their individual portfolios had ended up at about the same place. They each had felt their own measure of stress in different ways: hers stemmed from the volatility in the market, and his from his indecision on whether to reenter it.

Both would have benefited greatly from a strategy to protect them in the early stages of an emergency and to signal when it was wise to invest again. They needed a process and a discipline to overcome their emotions. Risk-Adjusting Portfolios™ strives to do just that. Indecision and regrets play a diminished role. You know what to do. You have a discipline for any season, whatever the season.

Does this really work? Our latest information and research will be on our website. Please go to TheForeverMillionaire.com for the latest updates.

Partial Truths That May Not Help

In 2016 we heard more and more that the S&P 500 Cap Weighted Index (in which large companies have a bigger share of the index) would beat every other investment option. *Remember our point about popularity, the news cycle, and prices rising and falling.* Morningstar's research indicated that the index has outperformed 80 percent of actively managed funds recently, and other time periods show different percentages.[10] However, the research compared the S&P 500 Index only to actively managed funds in the Morningstar database. The vast majority of mutual funds in that database are restrained by their prospectus from doing anything more active than selecting from stocks in their specified segment of the market. The active portion is picking and choosing stocks, but they cannot choose something else that might be safer, like a money market fund for example.

How active is that? The comparison did not include actively managed strategies involving investments that were not mutual funds or ETFs from their database. Still, people embrace such

---

10   Matias Möttölä, "Global Briefs," *Morningstar Magazine*, December/January 2017.

reports even though they don't stand up to examination. It's easy for Warren Buffett to say, as he did a few years ago, that he would want 90 percent of his widow's retirement fund to be invested in an S&P 500 Index, with the rest in short-term government bonds. He didn't make his fortune that way! And his widow will never need to worry about money. She probably could survive a 50 percent loss and wait five years to get it back. But could you?

In our review, the S&P 500 Index that many commentators suggest you use might not even be the best S&P 500 index for you. Let's look at the results of four ways to index and use those same five hundred stocks:

S&P 500 Cap Weighted Index—Bigger companies have more weight, just as bigger states get more congressmen and women in the House of Representatives.

S&P 500 Equal Weight Index—All five hundred companies have equal weight, just as each state gets two senators.

S&P 500 Dividend Aristocrats Index—Out of the five hundred companies, this index owns the ones that have raised their dividend for the last twenty-five years.

W. E. Donohue's Power Dividend Total Return Index—Buys the five highest dividend paying stocks in all ten GICS sectors once per year. Will sell all stocks and go to money market based on a risk overlay.

Here is a ten-year comparison of the four different indexes:

	TEN-YEAR RETURN AS OF JAN. 3, 2017**	LARGEST LOSS OF VALUE DURING TEN YEARS	TIME TO GET BACK TO PREVIOUS HIGH
S&P 500 CAP WEIGHTED INDEX SPX	7.05%	-56%	65 months
S&P 500 EQUAL WEIGHT INDEX SPW	8.53%	-60%	54 months
S&P DIVIDEND ARISTOCRATS INDEX	9.76%	-51%	47 months
W.E. DONOHUE'S POWER DIVIDEND TR INDEX*	13.48%	-12%	15 months

For illustrative purposes only.
*We currently use an investment vehicle that seeks to mirror the Power Dividend TR Index for many of our clients as well as one or more of the other three indexes from time to time.
** All data was found at spindices.com on Jan. 3, 2017.

The first three indices stay invested in their stocks all the time—no matter what the current market conditions are—based on their respective ways of using those five hundred stocks. The last index, Power Dividend Index, is an example of using simple technology improvements, sorting for dividends annually, and using a moving average signal to go to safety. It strives to reduce risk during market downswings, to shorten the time it takes to bounce back to previous levels, and to be invested in rising markets. The idea is a strategy that can adjust to market conditions as they happen instead of managing for the average market risk over the last twenty to thirty years.

We believe you and most investors could benefit from knowing more about strategies like this and how a prudent, proactive risk management process could prevent large losses. In other words, how would you feel, what would happen to your confidence if you could eliminate severe winter seasons from your portfolio?

We have included one example here as a way to look at markets differently. There are more examples on our website at TheForeverMillionaire.com.

With that as a backdrop for a potential game-changing investment process, do we still see reasons to use other types of solutions or products?

Yes, when they work as we outline here.

Caution on Commissionable Products

In general, every product or investment possibility can be a good one if four conditions are met:

1. It fits in with your financial planning, values, and goals.

2. It solves the right problem.

3. It is not loaded up with commissions and fees that cut your return and typically make it less liquid (i.e. you have some kind of restriction against getting your money whenever you want).

4. You do not give up too much control to someone else, resulting in your interests not aligning—for example, a real estate management team that could load up a REIT (real estate investment trust) with a lot of debt, causing losses or lower returns.

One of the knocks about annuities (although the same goes for all those other potentially high load/commission products) is that they are oversold and used as a solution to every problem. Typically, they pay some of the highest commissions, the compensation is not transparent, and you tie your money up for five to sixteen years or more. Annuities are sold mostly for their guarantees against market declines. But if you take a different approach such as the one we have outlined in this chapter, you may look at them differently.

Annuities are awesome when used to solve the right problem—and that's usually when you need guaranteed income. We have used them over the years when we find really good terms for clients. But some "advisors" only sell annuities and are not licensed to use stocks or bonds or similar investments. We have seen investors with all their money in annuities, which seldom makes sense. What we see many times when investors are unhappy and looking to find a better solution is that they are loaded up with annuities and other products with a larger commission. No matter how you slice it, when you pay more in commission, you have less money to go to work for you.

Investors are sold a "product" that gives the salesperson the incentive of an upfront commission. The salesperson and the firm get all their money now, but as the investor, you are usually tied into a long-term commitment and have to wait to see how it works out. If you wait six years and lose money, you hear this: "Well, we can't control the market." And here may be the biggest problem: Would an advisor working on commission want to show you an option that looks great now or one that's had a rough couple of years? Something with a recent good track record of course—which can also lead to buying high and selling low. And when something is doing poorly, causing you pain, your advisor can always have a solution that will look and feel better to you because you sell that ugly thing and buy that better looking one—again, potentially helping you sell low and buy high, all while making a commission. Imagine that.

But what if you only bought investments that were fully liquid every day and you didn't have to worry about being stuck with something you didn't like or want? You could have a more effective risk management process: at the first action point of your risk management discipline, you could liquidate or change and avoid more trouble. This is more of what we advocate as the core of your investment philosophy. You retain complete control.

Ultimately we believe it is the use of different strategies and asset types that will help you manage risk and diversify well. A tailored plan using the right tools and solutions for you should get you the best result. We help you by using services that help us search the entire market for these products so that you get the appropriate fit instead of someone else getting a better commission.

Here is a partial list of products where commissions can play a factor and you could get better terms or lower fees by comparing all the available options:

- annuities

- life insurance

- long-term care insurance

- disability insurance

- heck, let's just say *all* insurance

- private/non-traded investments of all kinds

- structured products, typically FDIC-insured but with additional income tied to growth in an index of some kind

- municipal bonds

- let's just say *all* individual bond options

- mutual funds

- wrap programs

- online asset allocators

—————— T H I N K I N G   P O I N T S ——————

1. Do you understand the investing trade-offs from recommendation to recommendation?

2. What are your beliefs about risk management? Do you want to take huge risks to make a better return?

3. Would you have more peace of mind if you knew someone was watching over every position in your portfolio 24/7 and had a written process to take prudent action on your behalf?

4. How can you learn to harvest in fall, buy in spring?

CHAPTER 6

DRAGS ON YOUR PROGRESS

One of the long-held fish stories in the financial media is that fees are the heaviest drag on a portfolio's returns. The same loose conglomeration of facts is used to tell and retell the same story: high fees will cost a huge percentage of the overall return, and they are the single biggest worry.

The story usually includes some version of a Morningstar report that finds that up to 80 percent of "actively" managed funds do not beat their index benchmark. The investor's natural conclusion: always buy the index and save extra fees. The story has grown to suggest that since investors can't beat the market, they should just buy and hold forever, since any fee will reduce returns.

As with any good fish story, the size of the catch is also up for debate. The financial media often use a version of the same infographic to show how much it costs. A 7 percent annual compounded return versus a 7 percent annual compounded return with 2 percent deducted, leaving investors to conclude: saving the fee is the most important goal.

Don't get us wrong. Fees are important, but we are not here to perpetuate fish stories. No market or investment has made 7 percent compounded annual return in a straight line for a significant time frame that they show as proof. It could just be BS—blatant self-interest. However, depending on your situation, fees could be only one of the factors that are eating away your returns.

In this chapter, we will share strategies for overcoming five of the biggest drags on your portfolio's progress:

1. Letting the market manage your money.

2. Paying fees or commissions for the wrong thing.

3. Not paying attention to taxes, or conversely letting taxes drive your whole investment plan.

4. Falling for dumb ideas.

5. Not learning from your mistakes.

Letting the Market Manage Your Money

Who, or should I say what, is really managing your money? The typical client/advisor relationship involves the client allowing the advisor to manage his or her money and the advisor putting the client's money in a cookie-cutter portfolio that goes up when the market goes up and goes down when the market goes down. While I realize that doesn't sound all that unusual, it's simply because the problem is vast—it is the market that is really managing your money.

And how much special care and attention do you think the market is giving to your money? The bottom line is that the market doesn't care about you, your money, or your future.

What about simply having someone truly manage your money to avoid the winter season? Do you think the market is going to do that? Think again.

Paying Fees Or Commissions for the Wrong Thing

When it comes to fees, the most important question is this: "What are the results after fees?" It certainly is necessary to consider fees when weighing investments, but should fees be the most important part of the decision?

Above all, your fees need to be completely transparent. You should know what you are paying your broker, your insurance agent, your financial advisor. And consider the type of fees and the incentives involved. Are you paying an asset-based fee or a commission? Salespeople on commission don't feel much of an incentive to be on your side of the table.

The fee that we charge our clients for managing their assets is fully transparent. That is not necessarily the case for many of the fees within mutual funds, even those fees that are listed in the fund prospectus. Annuities, too, contain charges that you might not see.

The point is that fees are a part of investment life. Money managers understandably will want compensation for what they do. Many fees are fair and reasonable, but some become a major and unnecessary drain on the return. The fees need to be fully disclosed and clear so that you know what you are dealing with and how much they will cost your portfolio. If you are paying a higher fee, you should expect a higher level of service.

Before we leave the topic of fees, let us add this point: If you have an IRA, normally you can't deduct the fee from your taxes. If you are paying the fee with non-IRA funds outside of the account itself, the amount that you pay is tax deductible after you meet certain thresholds on your tax return. The amount that you pay a fee-based advisor also can be deductible, within certain restrictions.

Many people do not realize that they can do that. It's an example of money falling through the cracks, year after year. A lack of understanding and knowledge prevents people from taking full advantage of all their tax-saving options. A good advisor can help to identify opportunities large and small where you can save on how much you need to send to the government.

Not Paying Attention to Taxes

Unfortunately, there is not all that much that can be done about income tax for people still in their working years. They are not about to ask that their employer pay them less to keep their taxes low. Instead, they make as much money as they can and try to defer paying some of the taxes, typically through a defined contribution plan such as a 401(k) or IRA. In their retirement years, however, they can have more impact on how the investments that they withdraw are taxed—that is, if they plan effectively.

Those who use the right strategy can save significantly on their taxes by withdrawing their income from a combination of taxable, tax-deferred, and tax-free accounts. The investments within each account need to be properly positioned for greatest tax efficiency. That way, retirees are able to manage the tax bracket and remain at the lowest possible rate while still producing sufficient income for a comfortable lifestyle. By controlling that income level, they also can realize other advantages, such as staying below the threshold where they will have to pay significantly more for Medicare Part B.

We once were approached by a retiree in her early seventies who had been withdrawing more than she needed each year from her retirement plan, figuring it would be nice to build up some savings in the bank. She now had reached the age when her withdrawals weren't voluntary anymore. The IRS required a minimum annual distribution—but only half as much as she had been taking.

When she came in to see us, we pointed out that her excessive withdrawals were worsening her tax burden, pushing her into a higher bracket. She was amazed at how high her taxes had become. "I don't need to be taking that much out," she said. "I could do just fine on half that much." And that is what she decided to do. She still met the minimum distribution, and her tax bill fell dramatically.

We often work with our clients on strategies to sell portions of their portfolio in a way that keeps their taxable income from rising to a higher bracket. Tax management is essential in a comprehensive financial plan, because taxes can be a major drag on the performance of a portfolio.

Tax management should also include a close look at all the available options in 401(k)s, IRAs, Roth IRAs, and other retirement plans that offer tax advantages. What is the most tax-efficient way to set up all your different accounts and to take advantage of them fully? Tax-deferred accounts, used properly, can offer huge tax advantages over the years, but often employees will fund their 401(k) only to the point where it continues to get a matching contribution from their employer.

Roth IRAs also can play a major role in retirement planning. Unlike a traditional IRA or 401(k), the Roth does not offer an up-front tax deduction for the amount of the contribution in the year that it is made. It does, however, offer a significant benefit during retirement: when the money is withdrawn, it comes out free of taxes (assuming certain criteria are met). This tax-free source can help retirees attain a higher income level while the taxable amount remains in the lower brackets. It also is a means of leaving money to heirs without subjecting them to a tax burden.

In recent years, a lot of companies have been offering Roth 401(k)s as an option for their employees. Most of those employees, however, are confused about how to take advantage of that opportunity. A big advantage, besides the tax-free benefit for retirement, is this: the contribution limit is much higher for the Roth 401(k) than it is for the Roth IRA. You potentially could put as much money into a Roth 401(k) as you put into a traditional 401(k). If you contribute to both, you will be receiving both a tax-free and a tax-deferred benefit on portions of your overall portfolio. You will be producing a pool of retirement money from which you will be able to withdraw in a tax-efficient manner. And if you are a business owner, you might want to establish the Roth 401(k) option to benefit yourself as well as your employees, so that you, too, can take advantage of tax-free savings, even at your higher income.

Many people, upon hearing about the relative advantages of the Roth IRA, are interested in converting their traditional retirement plan into a Roth. To do so, they would need to pay the deferred taxes upon making the conversion. This can be a tricky process, and people often make mistakes. Whether a conversion would make sense for you would depend on your unique income and tax situation, your age, and how you intend to use the money, if at all, in retirement. You should only undertake a conversion with professional guidance, making sure that you have fully examined every angle and possible consequence. A Roth conversion can be a valuable strategy, but not necessarily for you. Each set of circumstances is unique.

The other thing we see happen a lot is people will not take needed action in their portfolios because they would have to pay taxes. It's the tail wagging the dog.

You should always be conscious of tax consequences when making decisions. But as an example, suppose you have $1 million in unrealized gains on your $2 million stock portfolio—and it's 2007. Now suppose that your prudent, savvy advisor suggests that you get very, very conservative because there are meaningful, reliable indicators that suggest a severe winter is around the corner and your stock portfolio would likely get decimated. But to follow your advisor's advice, you'd have to sell your stocks—those stocks you have $1 million in unrealized gains—which means you'd owe the government capital gains taxes on $1 million in *realized* gains. Let's assume that you're in the highest tax bracket and your long-term capital gains rate is 20 percent. Your tax bill would be $200,000 if you sold your stocks! Would you do it?

Well, if you didn't, you likely lost $1 million in the ensuing winter cycle that was the Great Recession of 2008. The $200,000 you didn't pay in taxes cost you $1 million in your portfolio losses in this example, as the value of your portfolio was cut in half.

If you did go ahead and sell, hypothetically, you're sitting with $2 million in 2008 deciding what to do next. Effectively, a $200,000 tax bill saved you $1 million.

Don't get us wrong; there are times when it's simply better to not sell. Sometimes it's because the tax bill would outweigh any potential upside from selling. Or another example is in the case of extremely elderly investors who have taxable accounts (e.g. trust accounts) with large unrealized gains. In these situations there's the potential for a step-up in tax basis at the death of the first spouse. That means that all the unrealized gain in the portfolio goes away at the death of the first spouse, and liquidating a portfolio of stocks that had $1 million in unrealized gains now has $0 in unrealized gains.

A good advisor will know and be able to counsel you on when it makes sense to even consider paying taxes to shift your portfolio around and when it doesn't.

Falling for Dumb Ideas

People have a way of neglecting to check things out. Ideas that sound good at the time can turn out to be unwise, and yet the dreamers and the schemers continue to attract investors. We call this threat to portfolios the "drag of dumb ideas." They are not necessarily devious, although they might be—the Bernie Madoff scandal comes to mind—nor are they necessarily illegal. They just might not be right for you, and somebody may need to help you see why.

Vanguard authored a report in September 2016 saying that a good financial advisor is worth about 3 percent per year.[11] A big part of that 3 percent is attributed to the advisor's ability to keep the investor from doing the wrong thing. A Morningstar study from 2013 determined the worth of an advisor to be about 1.8 percent per year.[12] Again, it found that a big reason for that value is that the advisor keeps the investor from pursuing a dumb idea and/or optimizes the investor's entire financial resources to meet the investor's personal goals.

Numerous times we have talked people out of those ideas, or at least tried. A professional shelled out $100,000, for example, so that one of his children could start a business—and the money quickly disappeared. Sometimes the dumb idea is a questionable enterprise, or a shaky investment, or a risky strategy; and sometimes it is the tendency to wait until the market hits the bottom and then bail out, never to return. So many people focus on whether they are paying the lowest fee possible, but fees are hardly the greatest threat to a

---

11   Francis M. Kinniry Jr., Colleen M. Jaconetti, Michael A. DiJoseph, Yan Zilbering, and Donald G. Bennyhoff, "Putting a value on your value: Quantifying Vanguard Advisor's Alpha," Vanguard, September 2016, https://www.vanguard.com/pdf/ISGQVAA.pdf.

12   Michael Kitces, "Morningstar Tries to Quantify the Value of Financial Planning - 1.8% Gamma for Retirees?" Kitces.com, November 12, 2012, https://www.kitces.com/blog/morningstar-tries-to-quantify-the-value-of-financial-planning-1-8-gamma-for-retirees/.

portfolio. Good advisors will cost considerably less than what they can help their clients make or save. Often, they save people from themselves.

You hear a lot about where you can get free financial advice, but you need to ask what that advice is actually worth. The adage "you get what you pay for" holds so true. If you are using an advisor who is going to put you in a diversified market portfolio and just "let the market manage your money," then you should shop for the lowest price. You might even do that yourself and save any fee. Instead, you should find an advisor who will really manage your money, have your best interests in mind, help you know what you don't know, and work with you as a team to achieve the result you want.

SAVING MORE THAN THE IRS GETS

—Dave

Until I was in my midtwenties, I harbored the naïve belief that everybody was wealthy by the time they got to retirement. My early experience in working with seniors opened my eyes. I soon realized that the way to become wealthy was to save first and spend second.

Over the years, I came to see another truth: the better I was doing financially, the more I had to pay in taxes. That did start to affect how much I could save, and I did see clearly how much taxation could drag down a portfolio.

And so I set another goal for myself. Not only would I save first and spend second, but I would always save more for myself than I sent to the IRS. That certainly can become an ever-increasing challenge as your income grows. If you are sending 30 percent to the IRS, and you also want to save 30 percent for yourself, then you are living on only 40 percent. That is what I resolved to do, and that discipline made a huge difference.

Taxation serves an essential function in our society, but it must be carefully managed within the portfolio so that we do not pay more than our fair share. Similarly, investment fees can be another drag on the portfolio, but they are not without purpose—and it is up to the individual to determine whether they are fair and yield more than they cost. Good portfolio management is a matter of making wise decisions—and steering clear of dumb ideas.

Not Learning from Your Mistakes

Okay, so I know we've all heard the quote that doing the same thing over and over again and expecting a different result is the definition of insanity. The thing is, when it comes to money, many people who don't do as well as they'd like make the same mistakes over and over again and don't learn from them.

To be successful, one of the most fundamental principles to get right is to buy low and sell high—more often than not, unsuccessful investors do the opposite. And it all comes down to their emotions. Most unsuccessful investors buy high because they're driven by greed, thinking they're going to miss out on the next big thing. Most unsuccessful investors sell low because they're driven by fear, thinking that prices are going to keep dropping after falling already. A lot of times, they're the last ones to sell.

It's easy to look back after going through this with a stock or some other investment, but how about when you change advisors when the advisor has not delivered results? People switch advisors all the time because they're not satisfied with the results, but they're usually going from an advisor who hasn't done well to an advisor who ostensibly has done better. But unsuccessful investors fail to realize this is just another version of selling low and buying high. Unfortunately, some advisor/client relationships don't have a solid foundation from the beginning. They're usually a result of the investor being friends or acquaintances with the advisor and thinking to themselves, "I know this person. I trust them more than I'd trust someone else I don't know. I'll ask them for help with my money."

This leads us to the concept of attribution theory. In his book *Smartcuts: The Breakthrough Power of Lateral Thinking*, Shane Snow discusses how people tend to attribute factors that contribute to their success to themselves, but attribute factors that contribute to their failure to external factors. And because of this, it's really hard for people to learn from their own mistakes—since they don't attribute their mistakes to themselves, they feel there's nothing they need to change. The reason they succeeded was their skill or smarts, but the reason they failed was bad luck, or someone else's actions, for example. This happens with unsuccessful investors, too. They just don't realize their mistakes to begin with!

So how can you solve this? Work with a trusted advisor who can keep you accountable when you start going down the road of wanting to making the same mistakes you did before.

The key to eliminating drags on your progress is to work with a trusted advisor who can guide you around the pitfalls we discussed in this chapter. The cost of an advisor *could* be a drag on your progress, but we suggest working with an advisor whose fee is completely made up for by the value they create for you. A good advisor should be able to help you navigate tough markets, keep your fees down, and let you know where the hidden costs are. They ought to be able to coordinate with your tax professional to help you minimize your taxes and know what nuances you need to pay special attention to. And finally, a good advisor ought to be able to help you from falling for dumb ideas and hold you accountable on learning from your mistakes.

———————— THINKING POINTS ————————

1. Do you understand all of the fees you are paying with your current advisor?

2. Are you aware of the impact your decisions have on your taxes?

3. Do you conduct proper research before following up on a particular investment tip or strategy?

CHAPTER 7

TAILORED SOLUTIONS

Everyone looks better in custom-tailored clothing, right? But while tailored clothing might not be worth the expense to you, a tailored financial solution doesn't have to cost more, though it might take a little more time and thought. We think everyone should have organized strategies. Your financial plan should fit well.

You may have tried to solve the popular puzzle Rubik's Cube, twisting and turning layers of squares so that all of those on each face are the same color. If you resisted the urge to hurl the cube against the wall in a moment of multicolored exasperation, you eventually may have solved the puzzle, even without peeling off and rearranging the colored stickers.

The financial lives of many people come to resemble the Rubik's Cube. A variety of complex moving parts, intricately connected, can be exceedingly difficult to get in a row. The mix-and-match world of financial products can be maddening without some clues on how to line them up to work best for you. It's a puzzle you must solve, and this one isn't merely for fun. Your dreams may depend on it.

Working to solve the financial planning puzzle brings a sense of relief as you get things in order and know that you have attended to important concerns. And it all must work in concert. The goal is harmony. You want to get the colors of your life into proper position so that you need not worry about them. That's what we do for our clients: we offer abundant hints and guidance toward solving the puzzle.

EATING OUR OWN COOKING

—Dave

As an insurance salesman early in my career, I enjoyed working with many sharp older people but recognized that occasionally I was dealing with people of diminished capacity. My heart went out to them. I also recognized that among my colleagues in town were a few competitors whose heart wasn't quite in the same place. I met couples who already had four or five policies, and agents were going back to the trough, trying to sell them more.

The insurance industry is important and progressive — but I did meet a few opportunists who gave that industry a bad name. I can think of two of them who I heard ended up in legal trouble for one reason or another. I wasn't surprised.

We try to abide by the simple rule — you might call it a version of the golden one — that we should only do for our clients what we would do for ourselves if we were in their shoes. We would not invest for clients in a way that we would find inappropriate for our own portfolios. That rule, of course, somewhat depends on age and circumstances — at my stage of life, for example, I would not want or need many fixed-income investments. My point is this: We believe in what we recommend. We eat our own cooking.

Long ago I assessed what I would want for my family if I were to die prematurely. Early on, I bought a $1 million term policy. It was inexpensive and sufficient when we were starting out. Later, as I built assets, I purchased more insurance. When our children were in their teens, I opened an irrevocable life insurance trust and put a ten-year term policy in it that would cover my children's college years.

A good friend recently lost her husband — and financially she is fine, thanks to a million-dollar term policy he bought to take care of her. It cost little but provided much. Insurance, when used appropriately to solve real needs and problems, is an indispensable tool. It protects against damage to home and property and against liability — and an umbrella policy can provide additional protection for families of high net worth. Insurance also can protect against disability and long-term care costs.

Just be certain that you are getting the right product for the right use and that you are buying protection that you truly need. Think it through. Do you really want to pay dearly for that extended warranty on a television set? Instead, you might want to focus your attention on life insurance that would take care of your spouse and family or that would pay the taxes on a vacation property so that your loved ones wouldn't have to sell it.

It is important that you work with a financial advisor who understands and cares about your situation so that you can analyze and identify whether you have a legitimate need and the extent of it — and then go shopping for the appropriate solution based on your need, not somebody else's. Everything in your financial plan should fit together. Many people will try to weigh in on what is best for you. Some will be right, and some will be wrong. A trusted advisor — one who will eat his own cooking — can help you sort it out.

Charting Your Course

Take a look at the following chart, showing seven broad areas of financial planning that we address with our clients. Glancing down the columns, you will see several aspects under each category. Each factor plays upon the others in intricate ways that can be hard to understand or anticipate. Financial planning can feel as complex as Ernő Rubik's challenge.

The chart reflects the daily concerns as we seek to give our clients the financial harmony they need. As you can see, we do a lot more than help with the investments. We help set our clients on course toward financial stability, freedom, and a comfortable retirement, with clear goals and income streams to match. We help them with their insurance needs, tax planning, and estate issues, and we coordinate the other professionals so that we all are on the same page.

Financial planning is not about any one of those seven categories, each of which could become a book in itself. It's about all of them working together, like well-oiled machinery. A trusted advisor with a breadth of experience and knowledge will keep the gears meshing smoothly. You might try to keep it all going yourself, like a master clocksmith, but seldom do we meet people inclined to do so. They want to free up their time for other things. We have met many people who know a lot about one aspect of financial planning but relatively little about others. They are, in other words, unbalanced in their approach. They would be far better off with a broad range of knowledge so that they could synthesize and apply it effectively, delegating to others any tasks that call for expertise.

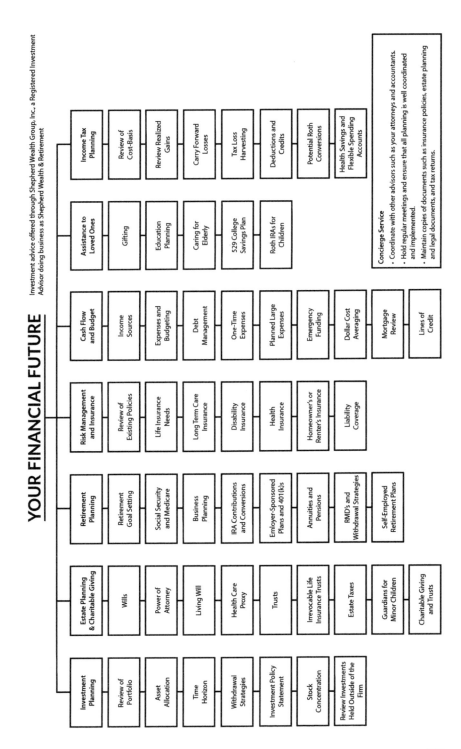

YOUR FINANCIAL FUTURE

Investment advice offered through Shepherd Wealth Group, Inc., a Registered Investment Advisor doing business as Shepherd Wealth & Retirement

Income Tax Planning
- Review of Cost-Basis
- Review Realized Gains
- Carry Forward Losses
- Tax Loss Harvesting
- Deductions and Credits
- Potential Roth Conversions
- Health Savings and Flexible Spending Accounts

Assistance to Loved Ones
- Gifting
- Education Planning
- Caring for Elderly
- 529 College Savings Plan
- Roth IRAs for Children

Cash Flow and Budget
- Income Sources
- Expenses and Budgeting
- Debt Management
- One-Time Expenses
- Planned Large Expenses
- Emergency Funding
- Dollar Cost Averaging
- Mortgage Review
- Lines of Credit

Risk Management and Insurance
- Review of Existing Policies
- Life Insurance Needs
- Long Term Care Insurance
- Disability Insurance
- Health Insurance
- Homeowner's or Renter's Insurance
- Liability Coverage

Retirement Planning
- Retirement Goal Setting
- Social Security and Medicare
- Business Planning
- IRA Contributions and Conversions
- Employer-Sponsored Plans and 401(k)s
- Annuities and Pensions
- RMD's and Withdrawal Strategies
- Self-Employed Retirement Plans

Estate Planning & Charitable Giving
- Wills
- Power of Attorney
- Living Will
- Health Care Proxy
- Trusts
- Irrevocable Life Insurance Trusts
- Estate Taxes
- Guardians for Minor Children
- Charitable Giving and Trusts

Investment Planning
- Review of Portfolio
- Asset Allocation
- Time Horizon
- Withdrawal Strategies
- Investment Policy Statement
- Stock Concentration
- Review Investments Held Outside of the Firm

Concierge Service
- Coordinate with other advisors such as your attorneys and accountants.
- Hold regular meetings and ensure that all planning is well coordinated and implemented.
- Maintain copies of documents such as insurance policies, estate planning and legal documents, and tax returns.

117

You need tailored solutions. Consider everything that is involved: the solutions will be different for every individual and couple and family. We certainly could go into long discussions about everything on that chart, and we could offer general advice—but because it could only be general, it would be unlikely to suit you well.

By developing a relationship with an advisor who has a legal obligation to look out for your best interests, you can discover the right tools and the right approach for you. You will need different tools for different jobs. A jackhammer is great for breaking concrete, but ten out of ten doctors would recommend a scalpel as a better choice for surgery. Your advisor, by getting to know you and your specific needs, goals, and dreams, will make sure that you are properly equipped for the variety of tasks at hand.

Each tool must be matched to its purpose. You will want some investments for living expenses and short-term goals, for example, and those will need to be liquid and relatively safe. You will want other investments to overcome inflation and to meet longer term goals—and depending on your time horizon, those can be invested at somewhat greater risk to command a higher return. And those are just the tools of the investment world. You will also need insurance tools, estate planning tools, and tools for tax efficiency and retirement income. You may need tools for providing assistance to your loved ones, such as helping the grandchildren with their education expenses.

What's the right approach for you? Until a fiduciary advisor gets to know you and your family well, the only honest answer to that question is: "It depends." Don't look to your neighbor or a friend. The way they are building their financial house may be a poor design for yours.

We meet people all the time who are in different places in life and with personalities that run the gamut. The human connection is much of the joy of our job. Some come to us with pieces of their financial future already assembled, and others are just getting started. One gentleman came to us recently with a multimillion-dollar portfolio and a full list of all of his positions. He was open about his finances and open to seeking good advice. Another couple came in to talk and did not want to share how much they had saved. "It's kind of a secret number," the husband said. They did eventually tell us, but they started out with a closed-vest attitude that is not uncommon: many people are wary of talking about money with someone they have just met. We understand, but there's not much we can do until we break that ice. That's why we put such an emphasis on relationship—we want to get to know who you are, what you desire, and what you stand for. We build the connection, and we build the trust. Only then can we chart a course that will help you and uplift you.

The one-size-fits-all prescription that is so common in our industry is a recipe for failure. You deserve more than a cookie-cutter solution that somebody pumps out for profit. Your years have been rich and diverse in experience. You didn't become successful by following the herd, nor should you do so as you work toward your most important, lifelong goals or prepare for retirement. Your approach to financial planning should be as unique as you are.

A MATTER OF TRUSTS

—Dave

Our daughter Michelle is challenged with cerebral palsy. She has graduated from college and is able to drive and live independently—though there was a time when we were unsure whether her needs would be more severe.

Her situation is what led me to begin thinking about a special needs trust. Sometimes people hesitate to set one up out of concern that their child would lose government benefits, but that did not apply in our case. My concern was that the money set aside for her should never be drawn away for other purposes. And as I thought that through, this came to mind: Why don't I just do that for our two boys and grandchildren, also?

We then designed our trust so that the principal would never be distributed. We provided a means for withdrawals if a special reason was presented. Otherwise, our children would be able to invest the trust as they wished and take out income not to exceed an established annual percentage. We wanted our children to have financial security but also protection against anyone who might try to stake a claim on those assets.

The ways in which trusts can be designed to suit your situation are many and complicated. The rules differ among the states, and you certainly will need an attorney to set one up correctly. Suffice it to say that a trust is a highly valuable tool, particularly for families of higher net worth for whom a simple will is not enough. Trusts do much more than divvy up the goods upon death. They can offer a level of control over how your life's work will be put to use in future generations. They can protect against those so-called "creditors and predators" out there, and they can position the family wealth to keep taxation lower while enhancing the potential for charitable giving. Unlike a will, they also keep assets out of probate court, thereby saving significantly on costs and keeping private family matters away from public view.

As a key element of estate planning, trusts essentially make sure that things go where you want them to go. So much can go wrong as you plan your family's future, but there are many preventive steps and solutions. You need an estate plan designed especially for what you and your family are facing. It's best to go to a professional and explain what you hope to accomplish and let them work with you to figure out how to do it. You need help with this. Sometimes we accompany clients to meetings with lawyers just to interpret the language. Getting a trust set up is definitely complex, but for many families it is simply a must.

This Time Is Different?

As we pointed out earlier, the Wall Street types love the positive spin. "Just stay fully invested and don't try to time the market," they say. "You don't want to miss those great days just to avoid the bad ones!" They don't tell you the results of missing the worst days, nor do they explain that the best and the worst days often come side by side, offsetting each other.

Over the years you probably have heard all the claims. "The tech stocks have changed everything!" and "Real estate never goes down!" and "Those subprime loans are now contained!" and "Gold will be going to $5,000!" The four words that cost investors the most money are "this time is different." People like to think they are onto something new and big. Typically, it's more of the same.

It's only when you know the full truth that you can make better decisions. You must never glow about the good times without a firm grounding in history and an understanding of the cycles. Depending on where you take the snapshot along that cycle and how long you set the exposure, you can make a case for a dramatic rise or precipitous fall in the markets, or something in between.

We think differently about your investments, as we explained in chapter 5. You need to dress for the season and heed the forecast and then choose between your sweater, T-shirt, and parka. Likewise, your portfolio should be appropriate for conditions. The all-weather, tough-it-out approach will leave you, much of the time, out shivering in the cold. In your investments, as in all aspects of your financial planning and for retirement, you need tailored solutions.

Controlling What Really Matters

Yes, there are things in life that do matter that you simply cannot control. There also are things that you often try to control but that simply do not matter much. In the sweet spot lie the meaningful things that you have the power to do something about. You can cast your vote in an election, but the results are not yours to control. You might worry about the direction of interest rates, or the market, but you hardly hold the reins of the economy and world affairs. Your focus is better placed on how much you earn, spend, save, and invest. That's where you can take concerted action to do things better, but it's just a start. You also can take action for the betterment of your family and to advance your dreams.

Think of it this way: will the things that worry you now be anything that you care about in five years? You can free yourself from a lot of emotional baggage by taking that perspective. You will be able to pick out the kernels amid the chaff. You will be able to discern what matters more than money, enjoying your time on earth with gratitude and authenticity. This is not to say that money doesn't matter. Clearly it enables you to accomplish more in the world, but it must be kept in its place. If you make it your top priority, for its own sake, then your marriage, family, friendships, and health could suffer, and what then? What have all your dollars bought you? More dollars? We know a man who has amassed more resources than he ever will need, but his son will not speak to him. The point is not who's at fault. It's a relationship in need of healing, and healing doesn't come from the wallet. It comes from the heart.

A LEGACY IN SONG

—David

Almost every year since we began dating, I have written and recorded a song for my wife, Chelsea, at Christmas time. The more kids we have, the more difficult it has been to follow through on that every year but she does have a collection of ten songs now, each of which tells a story of a particular highlight or moment from that year.

Chelsea and I are both musicians, and the last Christmas song ended up being one we wrote and recorded together. This most recent song was just a fun song to teach our kids our telephone numbers and home address—and to make them laugh.

It's fun to listen to those songs, as they've ended up creating an archive of our lives together. Our kids now get to listen to them and, whether they know it or not, are learning the story of our lives. In fact, one of the songs was composed around the heartbeat of our firstborn, Olivia. My hope is that these songs end up being one way that the story of how Chelsea and I lived and loved is remembered by our kids and grandkids and even generations beyond.

THINKING POINTS

1. What comes to your mind if I were to ask you, even with all the success you have achieved to this point, what items you would like to be better in your financial life?

2. What comes to your mind right now that you would like to do better in your personal life?

TO THE GRANDCHILDREN

Throughout this book we have talked about the nuts and bolts of what we do for our clients. In the last chapter, for example, we touched on insurance and trusts, and certainly you need to pass on your assets efficiently to the next generation. That's a matter of high importance, but so is this: unless you pass on your values as well, it won't matter. We believe you can help your heirs avoid "inheritance trauma" and help your spouse when they are "suddenly alone" if there is love, heart, and values passed along with your assets.

In our experience, we have seen many situations where families are blown apart by the passing of parents and the inheritance process. We have heard and seen many cases where the quick receipt of a lot of money without preparation can hurt heirs and relationships between family members. It has also been sad to see surviving spouses struggle with finances they have never dealt with before at a time when they have lost their life partner and their "purpose" in life. There is no magic bullet for this, but we believe there is huge potential for helping them to do better. We have a defined process, The Suddenly Alone Game Plan™, that we use with clients to strive to do everything possible to make it as stress-free, problem-free, and uplifting as we would like it to be for them.

As we were thinking about what we wanted to share in this book, Maryann Shepherd—wife of Dave, mother of David—found a decade-old letter in a drawer. The paper was creased and the ink was fading, but the words had lost none of their power. This was a letter from a father, written shortly after his son's wedding, addressed to grandchildren yet to be born. At the top, these words: "Letter to grandchildren, August 2005."

We already had jotted down ideas for chapters, examining many of the elements that you have seen in these pages. We knew that we would be covering a lot of territory, due to the nature of comprehensive financial planning. But after we rediscovered that letter, we read it together, looked at each other, and nodded. We realized that it captured the essence of what we hoped to say in this book. We could write paragraph after paragraph—examining investments and risk management and all the rest—without communicating what that letter accomplished in a few pages.

The letter addresses a variety of questions: What is life all about? Why were you put here on earth? Often it is not until their hair is getting gray that people begin to entertain such long thoughts. What will be your legacy for your loved ones, including those who may not arrive until after you depart? Will you be leaving them a gift or a mess? You can avoid leaving the latter by attending to all those details—but you must also attend to matters of the heart. What is the point of building a multimillion-dollar portfolio if your relationships lie in ruins? You can sign the papers to divide your estate, but it's a shame when the estate divides the family. But what if you could teach your loved ones just some of the better ways to be more thoughtful about their money now and in the future with some of the ideas in this book?

It has been said that your two most important days are the day you are born and the day you find out why. When you are clear about your life purpose, making decisions becomes easier. All the details begin to make sense when you understand why you are bothering with them. That is what the children, the grandchildren, and generations beyond need to know if they are to carry on a legacy of success in all areas of their lives, not just with money.

We have emphasized in this book that unbridled emotions can wreck your portfolio. But make no mistake: a lack of emotions can wreck your life. Investing in your family takes a lot of heart. Yes, you need to keep a cap on fear and greed as you manage your money. Living a life worth living, reaching your full potential, and helping others reach theirs requires you to pour out your heart and give it everything you've got.

Here, then, in our closing words, is that letter penned by one Dave Shepherd upon the wedding of son David to his yet-to-be-born grandchildren. It is more than a family keepsake. It is the heart of our message to you. Little did we know that we had finished our book before we started it. Writing this book was not easy, but, in the end, it was so very simple:

LETTER TO GRANDCHILDREN, AUGUST 2005

As I write this letter, my oldest son David has just gotten married and started his new life and family with a beautiful young lady, Chelsea. As I was watching the ceremony, I remembered his first breath when I watched him come to life at his birth. It's amazing to me how fast time goes and how we are going somewhere whether we plan to or not. Life is a lot of little decisions made every day that end up being the fabric of our lives. So if we are making choices every day that will make us or break us, how can we make decisions that will get us what we really want? I'd like to share a few ideas that may help you to be more successful.

By the way, how shall we define success? For purpose of our discussion, let's use being happy, content, and always moving toward bettering ourselves or others. Even if you don't have what you want yet, be happy and content with where you are now. God has a plan for your life, and one of the most important factors in growing into the person you are meant to be is overcoming the obstacles that come your way. If you can be happy in the face of obstacles and work until you overcome them, you will feel so much self-satisfaction and confidence that there will be no limit to what you can achieve. My daughter Michelle was born with cerebral palsy. I have never met anyone that wakes up with a smile and will face any challenge the way she does.

All the knowledge in the world is available for your use. Become a good reader. Men and women have worked lifetimes figuring out how things work and then document-ing it so you can learn it in a few hours. The best book in my mind is the Bible. The God who set up the planet tells you personally how it works. There is no end to what you can learn or how far you can go if you are curious and you can read and learn. Get an education and then further that education in what you enjoy. Make lifelong learning your highest priority.

Work hard, be diligent first, and you will have more free time. I've seen many take it easy and think, "When I need to,

I'll work hard." Trouble is you make laziness a habit and you can't change it later. Remember those decisions we make every day. Those become habits and then become unbreakable. Nowhere in all the reading I just suggested will you find laziness or lack of diligence to be something that will get you success or happiness. In fact, it may be the most destructive habit in life.

Many things in life are counterintuitive. If you are diligent and work hard first on whatever you are attempting, if you never give up when obstacles appear, if you work with passion and joy, you will always get done on time or earlier. It will always be complete, and you will always feel an incredible sense of satisfaction. You can then take it easy for a while and reward yourself for what you've accomplished. Most importantly, you are weaving into the fabric of your life a very important habit: successful completion of everything you start. Finish what you start, do what you say you will, show up on time, be happy and polite, and you will separate yourself from the crowd.

When you make decisions, think longer term. The most important decision in life is who you will marry and raise a family with. I would suggest that if a decision is made too quickly based on the rush of passion, you may pay for it for a lifetime. Just the words "lifetime commitment" should give you pause. The longer you can keep sex out of the picture the better. Wait until marriage. Sex changes the emotions so much that you may not become good friends like you will need to be later. Think about it: You will wake up with this person the rest of your life—without a shave or makeup. If you are not really good friends, you are in for a long ride. I guess the good news would be that it will seem like you are living a really long time.

Also, remember you will be marrying their entire family. You certainly don't want these decisions made for you because you get yourself or someone else pregnant. Make all your decisions this way. The only short-term decisions there is is what to eat for this meal and what movie to watch, and even that is debatable. If you eat the same bad food forever, it will certainly affect your life, and whatever you put in your mind will be there forever.

The more something costs, the longer time frame you should think about owning it and making sure you will be happy over that time frame, rather than just immediately. The world is trying to sell you things or sell you on doing things for their own benefit. Slow down and make sure it is best for you. Make your decisions away from the pressure of the moment. Talk to your spouse, parents, or mentors and get their feedback. A wise man or woman has many advisors.

Save first, spend second, never spend more than you make, borrow money carefully and infrequently. Those who save first and control their spending always have plenty and are increasing their financial security with every paycheck. Those that spend everything they make and borrow more will always be controlled by those they owe and will always feel pressure and insecurity. Why would you work hard for years on end and put yourself in the position of being insecure and having to work more? Again, at least it will seem like you are living a long time.

Be patient; it won't hurt to wait until you have the money. Those who rush pay a high price. Don't try to keep up with others; do what is right for you and your family. You'll be surprised how many of those who look like they have it all lose it all when they can't make the payments.

Have integrity. Be honest with yourself, with your family, with business associates, and with anyone you meet. If you are dishonest, you have to start over on all your relationships as you burn those people around you. Honesty builds a reputation in business and all relationships that makes getting things done easier. You do more with less effort.

The best things in life are free. I know I used to think otherwise, too. Money is a tool that can be used for good or bad. If money is your god, you will never have enough. You'll be like the squirrel running on the wheel. There is no end to it and no reward. If your family or friends, people, are your top priority, then money can be put in a proper perspective.

No amount of money is worth the experience of helping coach all three of my children's baseball teams at once. I can't imagine having a job or business that would have had me traveling all the time and missing their lives. My biggest joy during some of our worst struggles was coming home to three heads popping up in the window yelling, "Dad's home, Dad's home." And, of course, spending the rest of the day having fun with them. One day my youngest son, Matthew, told me I was his "palerino." I can't think of anything with a higher priority than being your son's "palerino." Work to live, don't live to work.

If you want to sum up a rewarding life, it's when every year gets more enjoyable and easier. You are getting wiser because of your lifetime learning. You get a lot done because of your diligence and good work habits. You never give up on any challenge and get everything done. You make good decisions and your past good decisions make your life easier and more fun. With every paycheck or business deal, you are becoming more secure because you save first and don't overspend. And because you are honest and put people and relationships first, you are full of joy and satisfaction.

Life is simple, just not easy.

OUR SERVICES

Are you looking for an advisor who has your back and works for you as a fiduciary without the conflict of interest of fat commissions or big money influence?

Do you need an advisor who can help you with all areas of your life that money touches and affects?

Regardless of where you are in life and what you are seeking to accomplish, we trust we can help you. But we understand that talking to someone else about your finances can be stressful. So if you qualify, we invite you to claim your Financial Clarity Experience™—our 100 percent complimentary analysis of your financial situation and your portfolio.

And if you decide that you want to work with us, here is what we can offer you:

- **Lifestyle maintenance and enhancement:** We believe that money is a tool to be used to help you achieve your life goals and dreams. It should be your servant and not the other way around! But the stress and uncertainty that may surround every major financial decision can spoil the joy and confidence that having money should provide you.

- **Goal-based financial planning:** Besides creating a plan aimed to help you achieve your goals, we use a systematic approach designed toward maximizing your returns and striving to reduce the stress associated with managing and investing your money.

- **Financial risk review and coordination:** Very few things (if any) in life happen exactly as planned. So we take into consideration mishaps, emergencies, or a simple change of mind that may appear along your journey.

- That is why **professional advisor coordination and sustainability** is important. At Shepherd Wealth & Retirement, we have a multi-generational team that can provide you with the long-term execution of the customized plan we design for you.

- **We help you make sense of all your investment options.** We speak a language that you can understand—no fancy words or jargon.

And we don't stop there ...

- **We help you accurately measure investment performance,** so you know exactly how your money is doing and, if applicable, when it is **the best time and the best way to exercise your stock options,** so we can strive to make tax-efficient decisions.

And talking about taxes we also offer you ...

- **Tax coordination, planning, and structure:** This is extremely important, as it can have a huge impact on your net returns. It can also impact what you will leave behind, be it to charity, your children, or your spouse.

- **Estate continuance, coordination, and liquidity:** What would happen if the "money manager" in your family suddenly passes? Is there a well-coordinated transition plan in place?

Will/should your assets be in a trust?

- **Trustee advice and support:** This is key when dealing with the planning and execution of your estate plan.

- **Education for trustees, beneficiaries, and the next generation:** The generation that succeeds you requires financial education. More importantly, it is essential that you prepare your children for the effect your wealth will have on them. And that influence goes beyond dollars and cents.

- **Facilitating the transfer of your values and principles to the next generation:** We assist you not only in preparing your children who will be accessing your assets and their trusts but also in facilitating the development and implementation of your family's mission based on your values and principles.

- And a lot more ...

We would be happy to speak with you and together create a plan to address any of these or other financial topics that impact your life and the lives of those you love.

To schedule your complimentary Financial Clarity Experience™ contact us at:

Shepherd Wealth & Retirement
www.ShepherdWealth.com | 520-325-1600

And together we will work toward helping you grow and stay rich!

Dave and David Shepherd